Anna Del Conte on Pasta

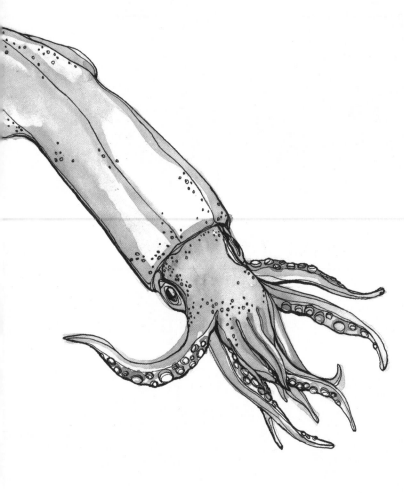

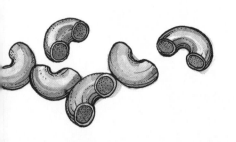

Anna Del Conte on Pasta

PAVILION

Acknowledgments

Many people have contributed to the making of this book and without their help I would never have achieved my goal.

First I want to thank Becca Spry, the commissioning editor of Pavilion, who decided to republish my *Portrait of Pasta* which first came out in 1976. I liked the book very much and I am delighted to see it in print again. *Grazie mille,* Becca.

Then *grazie mille* to Emily, my new commissioning editor, for all her hard work in guiding me through the difficulties of what to delete and what to leave and what to add and what to correct.

The copy editor, Maggie Ramsay, has been invaluable in the production of this revised edition and if this book is coherent and makes sense, it is due to her. *Grazie, grazie mille,* Maggie.

I am grateful to all the team at Pavilion, from Polly Powell, whose decision to republish my old *Portrait of Pasta* was essential, to Alison Legg, who produced the delightful illustrations and Laura Russell and Sophie Yamamoto, the designers, to Komal who has the task to make this book a 'best seller' (if she is able to make miracles), and everybody else. A big *Grazie.*

Grazie to Vivien Green, my agent, who is always at the end of the line, both land and electronic, to listen to me, encourage and support me and give me the right advice.

And last, but certainly not least, *grazie un milione* of times to my daughter Julia and my grandchildren, Nellie, Johnny, Coco and Kate, for testing, cooking, tasting, discussing and being bored stiff by Nonna and her pasta dishes. But I know they enjoyed it as well especially the eating and now, I hope, this new book.

From the 1976 edition:
I should like to thank the following people for the help and encouragement given me in the writing of this book.
Ing. Vincenzo Agnesi
Dr Lella Mariani, Rizzoli, Milan, Italy
Dr Corrado Sirolli, Fara S. Martino, Italy
Dr Livio Zupicich, Industrie Buitoni Perugina, Perugia, Italy

Contents

Introduction

Pasta knows no barriers of class or wealth. In Italy it is a favourite with princes and peasants alike (there such anachronisms still exist), and elsewhere in the world it may be part of a banquet or a simple supper. Pasta knows no national barriers either. Although a national dish – what other food is so strongly identified with one country? – it is eaten all over the world. Pasta is the simplest food there is – just wheat and water – and yet it can assume a hundred different guises, from cream to curry, from spinach to sardines. It is also the most versatile of foods, for it can be a first course, main dish, side dish or even dessert.

So read on. Find out about Yankee Doodle's macaroni, read the legends of miraculous macaroni, and discover what Lord Byron, Rossini and Sophia Loren have in common. And when you have read your fill, choose a sauce that suits your mood, boil up that saucepan of water and then, with due reverence, open up the package of pasta – or reach proudly for the pasta you have made yourself.

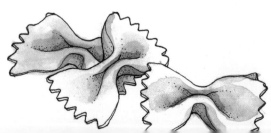

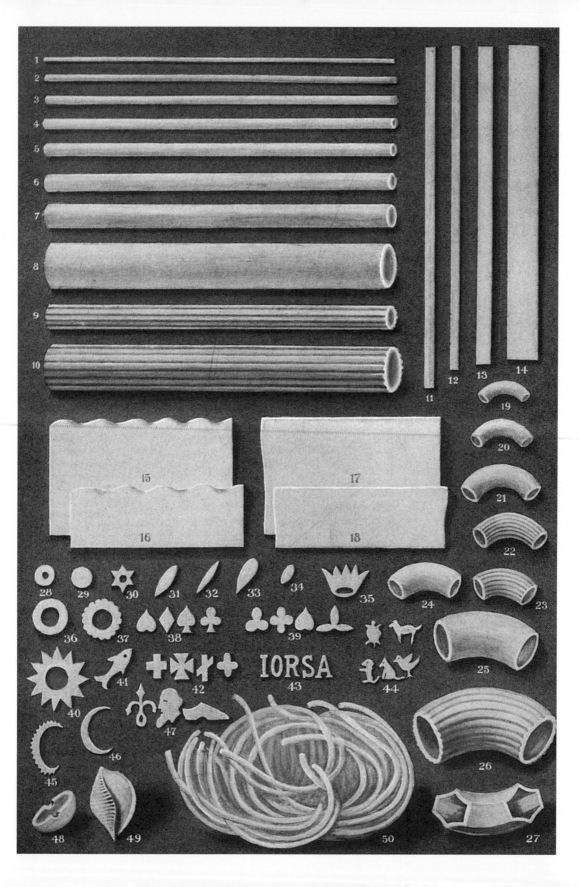

What is pasta?

What is pasta made of? What goes into its list of ingredients? Flour and water, that's all. Except that the flour used to make dried pasta is ground from durum wheat. Durum wheat – Triticum durum – is one of the many varieties of wheat, another being common wheat – Triticum vulgare – from which bread flour is made. It is called durum, the Latin for hard, because its grains are far harder than those of common wheat, and when ground, they produce a substance called semolina. Semolina is not powdery like flour, but instead has the consistency of sugar, and is made up of sharp, hard, amber-coloured granules.

A place called Taganrog

Durum wheat has grown in countries bordering the Mediterranean since antiquity. In the nineteenth century, however, Russia was one of the main producers of durum wheat, and Russian durum was known as the best. There was a big export trade in durum wheat to Italy for pasta making, and this centred on the port of Taganrog, on the Sea of Azov, which is linked by a narrow strait to the Black Sea. The fine durum wheat that was shipped to Italy was known as Taganrog wheat, and was the only wheat used by the best Italian pasta makers.

Durum wheat began to be grown on a large scale in Italy during the Fascist years, when Mussolini set out to make Italy self-sufficient. As part of his 'Battle for Wheat', 809,000 hectares (two million acres), many of them quite unsuitable, were planted with wheat.

Durum wheat today

Major sources of durum wheat today are the great plains and prairies of the United States and Canada. The grain grown there is not only used on the American continent, it is also shipped to pasta manufacturers around the world.

Meanwhile durum wheat is still grown in Russia and in Mediterranean countries, with Italy remaining the major European producer. But then that's not surprising for a country that is far and away the largest consumer of durum wheat in the world.

Above: Harvesting durum wheat on steep slopes in Tuscany, Italy.

Making pasta – then and now

There is a pleasing simplicity about how pasta is made. In essence, the grain of durum wheat is ground, the resulting semolina is mixed with water to make a paste, the paste is formed into the required shape and then it is dried. There are, of course, many refinements and subtleties, but these basic processes have been the same since pasta was first made and eaten.

Streams and stones

Mills and grindstones seem to have been a feature of civilization since the beginning of time, certainly since man has eaten bread – and pasta.

In Italy, the grain was washed in the millstream before it was ground. Women put the grain into wicker baskets, which they plunged into the water. Then they spread the grain out on the slate threshing floor to dry in the sun, and while it was drying they picked out the stones and other impurities.

Once dry, the grain was ground between two large round, ridged grindstones, lying flat one on top of the other. The bottom stone never moved, while the smaller top stone, which had a hole in the middle, turned on it. The grain was fed into the hole, and, when ground, it came out from the outer edge of the lower stone.

Modern milling

Today, the grains are still washed before grinding, but instead of wicker baskets there are carefully regulated jets of water. And instead of grindstones there are contra-rotating ridged steel cylinders into which the grains are pushed. At the end of the milling process, the resulting semolina still contains the husks and pieces of bran. To get rid of these, the semolina is purified in a device that uses air to separate the husks from the grain.

The end result is pure semolina, ready to be made into pasta. Ideally it should not have far to go, so that when used it is still fresh, and indeed most modern pasta factories are close to mills – often linked to them – in a position where centuries ago there stood the original mill astride its millstream.

Treading the pasta

The next stage is the mixing of the semolina with water to make the dough. Until about 1400, this time-consuming process was done only in the home. In most houses, although not those of the poor, there was a *madia*, a large trough in which the dough was kneaded. After long and laborious kneading in the *madia,* the dough was slowly rolled out with a rolling pin and then cut into strips or different shapes.

Over the centuries the production of pasta moved away from being a purely domestic undertaking. A register of the artisans of Savona, dated 1577, lists men occupied in making pasta, who were carefully graded according to levels of skill, from masters down to apprentices. By the seventeenth century pasta was being produced on a fairly large scale in 'factories'. But the way it was made was certainly not what that word suggests to modern ears.

A common way of starting the process of mixing semolina and water was with the feet, just as they tread on grapes to make wine.

Ferdinand II, King of the Two Sicilies from 1830 to 1859 and a notable despot, was shocked by this primitive method when he visited a pasta factory. He immediately ordered Cesare Spadaccini, a leading scientist of the time, to invent a better method of making pasta. At the end of a whole year's work on this

Above: 'Preparation of Pasta' in the fourteenth century Tacuinum Sanitatis Codex Vindobonensis (vellum), *Italian School.*

royal project, Spadaccini had drawn up elaborate plans for a model pasta factory, the high point of which was his answer to what he called 'the abominable practice of mixing dough with the feet.' Spadaccini replaced the live Neapolitan with an elaborate mechanical man, whose feet of bronze – robot fashion – trod the pasta in the accepted way. This was thought an excellent idea, and the building of a great factory began. But then the king lost interest, the money ran out, the factory was never finished, and human feet went on treading the dough for at least another fifty years.

Man-powered machines

All this treading only achieved the first stage of working a carefully regulated amount of water and semolina together into dough. After this the dough had to be kneaded to produce a really smooth, homogenous mixture. Until the end of the nineteenth century, and later in some small factories, the machinery for kneading the dough and for shaping it was often powered in various ways by men or boys – as shown on page 11. Human energy was transferred to the process in question by means of a long pole or a wheel. The dough was kneaded by repeated pummelling with the end of a wooden pole, or it was crushed by a rotating stone wheel. It was then put in a press, where a great screw bore downwards as it was turned, forcing the dough under extreme pressure against a perforated plate, or die. Forced through small holes, the dough finally emerged as spaghetti. These machines were made mostly of wood lined with bronze, the screw and plunger were also metal and the die was made of copper.

The turn of the screw

By the end of the nineteenth century, pasta was made largely by machines, albeit primitive ones, usually powered by steam or hydraulic power. There remained one barrier to speed and efficiency. In the press, the piston had to be drawn back each time, after it had forced the pasta through the holes in the die, so that another batch of pasta could be fed in.

It was an ordinary workman who finally saw a way round this block. Féreol Sandragné had worked most of his life for a Toulouse firm that made pasta-making machinery, so he knew the problem. When he retired, he took a job as a watchman in a brick factory to supplement his pension. There one day he noticed clay being carried forward and compressed by the threads of a helical screw, and as he watched, it turned to pasta in his mind's eye.

So he went home, and in his attic he made a working model of a continuous press for pasta in which the dough was carried forward in the threads of a screw, which then forced it through a die. In 1917 he invited his former employers to see the model. They were very impressed, and took out a patent in Sandragné's name, giving him a royalty on each machine they sold – the precursor of the modern machines.

Opposite top: Kneading machine for making vermicelli, c. 1880.
Opposite: Making macaroni in Russia fifty years ago.

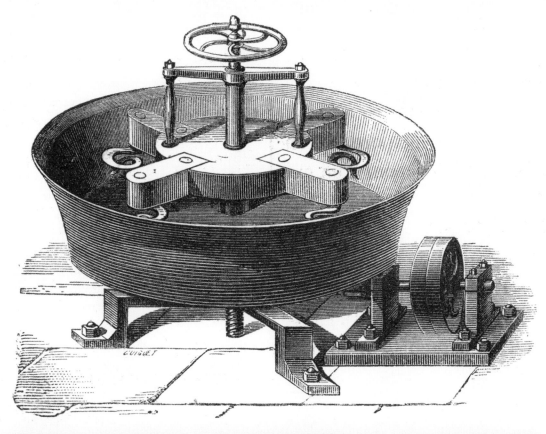

Sun and sea air

A notable Italian scene for smart young Englishmen making the Grand Tour in the eighteenth century was the spaghetti hanging out to dry in the streets of Naples. Outside a pasta factory the street would be lined with endless racks strung with spaghetti drying in the sun.

However, the drying process is by no means simple. If pasta dries too quickly, it will become very brittle; if it dries too slowly, it will go rancid. So it must dry neither too fast nor too slowly, and this was just what the climate of Naples made possible. Hot winds blowing off Vesuvius alternated with fresh sea breezes, and between them they provided perfect drying conditions for the pasta. The fact that two towns near Naples, Torre Annunziata and Gragnano, came to be – and still are – famous centres of pasta manufacture was largely due to the beneficial effect of these winds in the days when pasta was dried in the streets.

Modern methods

This story, which began with the millstone, sees the start of its last chapter in 1933 when Braibanti (well-known pasta manufacturers) patented the first machine to include all the stages of pasta making – mixing, kneading, extruding and drying – in one continuous process. Now we enter the era of automatically controlled production lines. The last stage of manufacture is no longer performed by the sun and sea air of Naples, but by automated drying tunnels.

Opposite: Pictures from the nineteenth century of spaghetti drying in the streets of Torre Annunziata and Gragnano.

Below: Women making pasta by hand in Tricario, Italy, c.1950.

Pasta through the ages

The history of pasta-eating is a fascinating subject. If its early pages are a little hazy, those of more recent times are full of amusing and interesting glimpses into unlikely backwaters of social history.

The mists of time

It seems certain that men have grown crops since the earliest traces of civilization, and that they were sustained mainly by eating the produce of these crops. Indeed one of the reasons why most ancient civilizations were situated in river valleys – those of the Tigris, the Euphrates, the Nile, and China's Yellow River – was that these were the most fertile places, where crops grew best.

These early people ate many foods that were made by crushing grains and mixing the resulting flour with water. In China, a fairly advanced civilization developed during the Shang dynasty (1700–1100 BC), and it is thought that one of their staple foods was a form of noodles. In that case, pasta's story starts almost 3,500 years ago. But not the story of my pasta.

The Greeks did have a word for it

In Europe, a clue can be picked up from the Greek word *laganon,* which means a broad flat cake, probably made with a flour and water mixture. Greek civilization flourished during the first millennium BC, so it is not unreasonable to deduce that pasta, more as a mixture of flour and water than as the ingredient we know now, goes back that far. Not only pasta itself, but also one of its many names, lasagne, since *laganon* led to the Latin *laganum* – mentioned by Horace in one of his *Satires,* and by Cicero, who loved to eat it. In Neapolitan dialect a rolling pin is still called a *laganatura.*

An Etruscan tomb

The next piece of evidence of pasta-eating dates from the fourth century BC. Central Italy, west of the Apennines,

was at that time ruled by the Etruscans, that mysterious people of unknown origin and undecipherable language. One of their main ports was Caere, about 50 kilometres (30 miles) north of Rome. All that now remains of this once-important naval centre is a large necropolis, where there is a tomb famous for its bas-reliefs showing everyday articles from an Etruscan home.

Carved on the two central pillars of the tomb are all the utensils for making pasta: a jug for drawing water, a knife, a rolling pin, a large board with a raised edge for keeping the water in when mixing it with the flour, a ladle for adding the water, a flour bag for dusting the board, and a pastry wheel.

In many parts of Italy today, more than 2,000 years later, you would find almost identical equipment for making pasta in most kitchens.

A Roman taste

In one of his *Satires*, Horace rebukes a friend, who is a judge, for not being able to go around the streets of Tivoli without five servants following him. For his part, he says, he goes where he pleases. 'I wander through the streets ... or often in the forum I stop at the fortune teller's. Then I go home to my supper, to a bowl of leeks, chickpeas and lasagne.' (My interpretation of this dish is on page 78.) Although the modern Italian for chickpeas is *ceci*, the Latin *ciceri* has been fossilized in the name *ciceri e trii*, still used for a soup of chickpeas and fried tagliatelle in parts of southern Italy. *Trii* is another revealing word, as explained below.

A few decades after Horace, there lived one Marcus Gavius Apicius, a Roman gourmet whose name became a byword for gluttony. A number of contemporary sources describe sensational stories of his love of food. Having eaten his way through a considerable fortune, he could not face the prospect of the lean days ahead, and poisoned himself. Whatever he did, a collection of recipes, called *De Re Coquinaria*, appeared under his name. In this there is a reference to strips of flour-and-water dough fried and dressed with honey and pepper. Another suggestion is for strips of dough cooked in oil and dressed with pepper and *garum*, a sauce made from the fermented entrails of mackerel, which the Romans seem to have splashed liberally on most things they ate.

Arab string

The gluttony of Apicius was in tune with the times. While Rome indulged itself in what today would be called 'an orgy of consumer spending', the outposts of its vast empire were being eroded by invasions from both north and south, and by the end of the first millennium the Roman empire had disappeared from the map of the world.

In the South, the Arabs invaded Sicily – and many other Mediterranean regions – and they brought with them a culture that was in many respects highly developed; they also introduced produce not yet known in the western Mediterranean countries.

In ninth-century Spain, under the Emir Abdurrahman II, there was a famous Arab minstrel called Ziryab. A novel feature of his songs was that they often spoke of food, of its attractiveness, and of the elegance with which it should be eaten. And among the foods mentioned are several that seem to be some kind of pasta.

At this time the Arabs were masters of Sicily, where their cultural and gastronomic influence persisted for a long time after the island was conquered by the Normans. The second Norman ruler of Sicily was King Roger II (1093–1154), and he commissioned an Arab geographer, Al-Idrisi, to explore the island and write a book about it. In this, Al-Idrisi writes that at Trabia,

near Palermo, he saw people making a food from flour, in the form of threads, which they called by the Arab word for string, *itriyah*. *Itriyah* became *tria*, and *trii* is to this day a word for spaghetti in parts of Sicily and other places in southern Italy.

This use of an Arab word clearly implies an Arab origin for spaghetti, but who is to know whether this *trii* antedated the Greek and Etruscan pasta? What it tells us is that pasta was eaten in different Mediterranean countries from the earliest times; its origins in the different countries were probably independent of each other. What is certain is that this pasta took many different forms according to how it was cooked. The most usual was for the dough to be fried or baked, and then eaten dry or in a soup. Indeed, to eat pasta fried was quite normal until the sixteenth century, and even when boiled it was often fried immediately afterwards.

Above: Pasta manufacture in sixteenth-century Italy.

Medieval macaroni

Some writers have said that Marco Polo introduced pasta into Italy after his twenty years' stint as a sort of Secretary of State to Kublai Khan. This is a pleasing romantic notion, but it does not square with the facts.

There is a reference to macaroni in a document dating from 1279, sixteen years *before* Marco Polo arrived back in Venice. In this 800-year-old document, which is in the Genoa city archives, there is a notary's list of the items left on his death by one Ponzio Bastone. Among these is a *bariscella piena de macaroni*, a basket full of macaroni. The contents of this basket are interesting for two reasons. First, this is the earliest known reference to what must have been dried pasta, as we know it today; secondly the fact that the macaroni was separately listed by the notary is an indication that it was something of a luxury, rather than an everyday dish.

The next medieval macaroni marvel is a great high mountain of grated Parmesan. In Boccaccio's *Decameron*, one of the stories is of the gulling of a simple soul. He is called Calandrino, and because he is simple his friends like to play tricks on him. So they tell him of some magic black stones he must collect in vast quantity and take home to his wife. To whet his appetite they describe a far-off place where the stones are to be found. There 'on a mountain, all of grated Parmesan cheese, dwell folk that do nought else but make macaroni and ravioli, and boil them in capon's broth, and then throw them down to be scrambled for.' Even in 1350 macaroni and grated Parmesan was something to tell stories about.

Francesco di Marco

By the fourteenth century, pasta had become a regular part of Italian life, albeit only within the upper strata of society. Scattered through documents of the period are references, for example, to a shop in Florence where pasta was made and sold; or to two pasta makers from Rome embarking on a galley where they were to keep the crew happy with fresh pasta during the voyage.

However, there is one particular source of information that gives a detailed insight into every aspect of Italian life at this time, including pasta. This lies in the incredible store of more than 140,000 letters written by the merchant Francesco di Marco of Prato in Tuscany, and still preserved in his house there. No wonder that he once wrote: 'I am not feeling very well today on account of all the writing I have done in these two days, without sleeping either by night or by day, and in these two days eating but one loaf.'

One loaf was not his usual fare, however, as Francesco liked good food and could afford it. He was particularly keen on the first course. This, as often as not, was lasagne or ravioli, and the stuffing of the ravioli consisted of pounded pork, eggs, cheese and a little sugar and parsley, after which the ravioli were fried in lard and sprinkled with sugar. During Lent the ravioli were stuffed with herbs and cheese and sprinkled with spices.

In the Tuscan city-states at that time, there were 'sumptuary' laws, which sought to restrain those with money from spending it too lavishly or ostentatiously. A banquet could consist of only three courses, but the Italians – then as now – were clever at getting around tiresome regulations. Thus the second course usually turned out to include a vast pie that was a gargantuan meal in itself. One such pie was made with chickens, sausages and ravioli filled with ham, which were laid on layers of pastry alternately with layers of dates and almonds, the whole being then covered with pastry and cooked in hot embers.

Renaissance riches

The Renaissance was so called because it was a 'rebirth' of the classical forms of art. In the culinary arts, too, Latin origins were studied, notably by Bartolomeo Sacchi. He had just been made head librarian at the Vatican, when in 1475 he published a cookbook that was to become a bestseller. Sacchi was a scholar, and the fact that he called himself Il Platina, after the Latin name of his home town Piadena, is an indication of his love of ancient Rome.

A remarkable sign of the great interest that there must have been in cooking in Renaissance Italy is the fact that between 1475 and 1500 his book, *De Honesta Voluptate et Valetudine,* went to nine editions, a large number for those days. Platina included many recipes for pasta, in one of which he specified that the pasta should be cooked 'for as long as it takes to say three Pater Nosters'.

The three-course feasts given by the merchant of Prato would probably seem like light meals compared to the vast and elaborate banquets given in the days of the Renaissance by the great families of Italy in their splendid palaces. In Rome, the Dorias and the Borgheses; in Ferrara, the Estes; in Mantua, the Gonzagas; in Milan, the Viscontis and the Sforzas; and last but by no means least – in Florence, the Medicis. When Lorenzo the Magnificent was married, he lived up to his name by giving a banquet a day for five consecutive days. Indeed, as even French historians will admit, Italian cooking was far and away the most highly developed in Europe at this time. Thus when Caterina, the fourteen-year-old great-granddaughter of Lorenzo, married the heir to the French throne in 1533, it was natural that she should take her Italian cooks to France with her. Fourteen was not so young for a bride then, and certainly old enough for her to have acquired in Florence the taste for extravagance and beauty. This she took with her to the French court, and in the new palace at Fontainebleau, in the Tuileries palace that she had built, as well as in her other Paris residence, the Louvre, Caterina gave sumptuous banquets *à l'italienne*. At these her Florentine cooks might well have served pasta to the nobility of France (I have never found any documented evidence). But the French never took Caterina de Medici to their hearts, nor did they adopt her national dish.

Above: Making noodles or pasta in a medieval handbook on health and well-being. Illustration from Ibn Butlan's Taqwim al-sihhah *or Maintenance of Health (Baghdad, eleventh century), published in Italy as the* Tacuinum Sanitatis *in the fourteenth century.*

A closed shop for pasta

By 1400 pasta had ceased to be a purely homemade product and was beginning to be made commercially. Like bread, pasta was sold in special shops and was made in the room behind the shop, as it still is in some village shops in the twenty-first century. As *vermicelli* was the usual generic word for pasta until the eighteenth century, a man who made pasta was a *vermicellaio*, and the shop he sold it in was the *bottega di vermicellaio*. The large room at the back contained the *madia*, in which the dough was kneaded, and the screw press for extruding it, and between there and the shop there was a courtyard for drying the pasta. In addition, so a contemporary document tells us, there was a bedroom for the night watchman.

The need for a night watchman is a reminder of the fact that, in the Renaissance period, pasta was still luxury food. It was eaten regularly by the wealthy, but for ordinary people it was food for feast days, weddings and other special occasions. As the manufacture of pasta became a trade of some importance, so its price was controlled by law. There are many records of proclamations issued in the various cities of Italy in the fifteenth and sixteenth centuries to specify the exact price per pound at which a particular shape of pasta could be sold. It is interesting to compare the official price of 40 centimes for the equivalent of a kilogram of pasta in Naples in 1670, with the official price of 400 lire for the same amount in October 1974. Perhaps one thousand-fold inflation in three hundred years should not surprise us too much!

It was not until about a hundred years after pasta was first made commercially that the *vermicellai* began to band together into *arti*, or guilds. They did so mainly to protect their interests against those of the bakers. The main point at issue was whether bakers should be allowed to go on making and selling pasta, something to which the *vermicellai* objected vigorously.

The controversy, which at times was nearer a battle, rumbled and raged throughout Italy – through the fifteenth, sixteenth and seventeenth centuries. Slowly the *vermicellai* won out, and an early sign of their increasing success and popularity was a Papal ruling in 1641 that there must be at least 25 yards between one pasta shop and the next!

Harlequinades and odes

It was another *arte,* this time the actors' guild or *Commedia dell'arte*, that gave pasta its first appearance on the Italian stage. In their improvised plays, so popular in Italy in the sixteenth, seventeenth and early eighteenth centuries, the masked actors impersonated the familiar characters of Harlequin, Columbine or Pantaloon, each with their stock phrases and actions. Prominent among the figures was Pulcinella, one of the servants or *zanni* (origin of the English 'zany').

Pulcinella's black mask had a hook nose, and he was a witty rogue as well as a practical joker. There was one thing that he seemed to be serious about, however, for whenever he appeared on stage he was eating voraciously from a steaming bowl of macaroni.

A seventeenth-century Neapolitan poet, Scruttendio. wrote an elaborate mock-heroic epic about pasta, *In Praise of Macaroni*. He also wrote a sweet little poem to his beloved, Cecca, from which the following is a verse.

> *Me deze no piatto Ceccarella*
> *de cierte sapurite maccarune,*
> *semmenate de zuccaro e canella,*
> *cosa da far sparire le pperzune.*

and in loose translation

> *My dear little Cecca, she gave me a plate*
> *Of macaroni delicious with a taste that*
> *   was great.*
> *All sprinkled with sugar and cinnamon*
> *   round about,*
> *So good when I ate it I almost passed out.*

Above: Pulcinella, stock figure of the Commedia dell'arte, *usually appeared on stage carrying his bowl of pasta.*

Naples supreme

So we reach the eighteenth century, when the story of pasta, until now somewhat episodic, is about to become history; its backdrop was Naples and its gulf.

Oddly enough, until about the middle of the eighteenth century Naples was known as the city of the *mangiafoglie* – leaf eaters. It was the Sicilians who, in the seventeenth century, had been the *mangiamaccheroni* – the macaroni eaters, and they had scornfully given the Neapolitans the name that came from their love of salads and green vegetables. (*Maccheroni* was at the time the name used for all kinds of pasta, spaghetti included.) By the late eighteenth century, however, the Neapolitans' love of leaves was to give way to the love of pasta. In 1700 there were 60 pasta shops in Naples, and in 1785 there were 280. Along with Vesuvius, pasta became the symbol of Naples. This was partly because, in this city where life has always been lived very much in the streets, pasta was a public spectacle. It was hung up to dry in the streets, it was cooked in the streets, and – most remarkable of all – it was eaten in the streets.

There were the long racks festooned with pasta, gently drying as the hot winds from Vesuvius alternated with the fresh breezes from the sea. If the drying racks outside the macaroni maker's establishment tended to be tucked away in side streets, not so the *maccheronaro* – the macaroni seller. There he was, at many a street corner, standing at his stall behind a charcoal stove and sheltered by a makeshift awning. On the fire was a pot in the shape of a top hat (still the best shape for cooking pasta) full almost to the brim with boiling water and macaroni. At his elbow was a gleaming white mountain of grated pecorino cheese, often topped by a small red flower or a tomato, and next to this a pile of plates. It was with his fingers that he placed the pasta onto the plates, and it was with *their* fingers that his customers ate it.

This is the characteristic Neapolitan scene, shown time after time in drawings of the period. A man, usually barefoot, stands next to the *maccheronaro*, his right arm raised, his fingers holding the pasta so that the lower end drops neatly into his upturned mouth. This everyday event in the life of the ordinary Neapolitan people soon became a tourist sight. Supercilious young English aristocrats doing the Grand Tour came to see the *mangiamaccheroni* eating pasta with their hands in the streets of Naples. And the *mangiamaccheroni* were always ready to demonstrate their technique for the price of a plate of pasta purchased by the watching tourist.

Late in the nineteenth century and in the twentieth century up to the time of the First World War, the production of pasta in the Naples area grew into what, for those days, was a giant industry. In the towns of Torre Annunziata and Gragnano, where the manufacture of pasta was centered, there was a spaghetti boom. On the coast at Torre Annunziata the ships from Russia discharged their cargos of durum wheat to be made into the pasta that was known throughout Italy as the best.

During the same period, from the port of Naples itself, very different ships were sailing to New York, loaded – and in many cases cruelly overloaded – with emigrants. Among the sparse belongings of all but the poorest families were several boxes of pasta, a reminder of home to help them face a new life in a foreign country. Hundreds of thousands of these new Americans kept the spaghetti boom going in Naples, not only by the boxes they took with them but also by the great quantity that was exported to meet their needs after they settled in their new homeland. And on almost every box was a label that reassured them that this was pasta as they knew it: a label bearing a picture of the bay of Naples, with Vesuvius rising above it topped by its plume of smoke.

Above: The macaroni sellers of Naples line up to have their photograph taken. The picture dates from about 1890.

Mangia maccheroni

Hands or forks

The eighteenth-century tourist who watched in wonder as the Neapolitans eased the pasta down their throats would have been surprised to learn that it was the Italians who, at least 300 years earlier, had been the first in Europe to use forks. A number of travellers commented on this. One of the earliest was a Frenchman, who in 1518 attended a banquet given by the Doge in Venice. 'The noblemen,' he reports, 'when they wish to eat, take the meat with a silver fork.' In 1605 an English traveller writes: 'At the table they touch no meate with the hand, but with a forke made of silver or of other metall.' Another wrote in 1611: 'I observed a custome that is not used in any other country that I saw in my travels, neither doe I think that any other nation of Christendome doth use it, but only Italy. The Italians doe alwaies at their meales use a little forke when they cut their meat. This forme of feeding I understand is generally used in all places of Italy. The reason of this curiosity is because the Italian cannot by any means indure to have his dish touched with fingers, seeing all mens fingers are not alike cleane.'

But forks were certainly unknown to the Italians of the backstreets of Naples – and, even if they were, it was far more picturesque to eat spaghetti with one's hands.

Opposite: Eating Macaroni (colour litho), Italian School, (19th century).

Travellers' tales

Italy, naturally enough, has always been a magnet for travellers. Sprinkled through their notebooks, diaries and jottings are occasional references to pasta.

An eighteenth-century traveller from England was Hester Piozzi, better known as Dr Johnson's great friend Mrs Thrale. In her journal *Glimpses of Italian Society*, Hester Piozzi wrote of a Neapolitan prince who seems to have captured her fancy. 'He shoots at the birds, dances with the girls, eats macaroni and helps himself with his fingers, and rows with the watermen in the bay.'

Our next traveller is Edward Lear, known for his nonsense verse and also as an artist. In 1852 he travelled as far south as southern Calabria, which not many Englishmen did at that time. In the journal he published he records an incident that happened while he was dining with the Caristò family at Stignano (a town right down on the toe of Italy).

A small juvenile Caristò, during the midday meal, climbed abruptly on to the table, and before he could be rescued, performed a series of struggles among the dishes, which ended by his losing his balance and collapsing suddenly in a sitting posture into the very middle of the maccaroni dish. Valentine cards often show Cupids on beds of roses, or on birds' nests, but a slightly clothed Calabrese infant sitting in the midst of a hot dish of maccaroni appears to me a perfectly novel idea.

Andrew Peabody was a nineteenth-century Harvard professor, who himself had graduated from Harvard at the tender age of fifteen. In later life he travelled to Europe and, in 1868, wrote about a journey to southern Italy:

'On our sunset passage back to Massa (near Sorrento) the promises of a macaroni supper bribed our boatmen to sing. Their voices were both sweet and strong and it may have been happy for us that they *were* strong; for we passed very near the rocks of the sirens, and if those maidens have not deserted their dwelling place, we needed a powerful counterspell to drown their seducing melody.'

'I left the maccaroni machine with my banker'

Thomas Jefferson was very much a Renaissance figure; he was the complete man. Statesman, philosopher, architect, writer, inventor – nothing was too great or too small to occupy his attention. And the interest he took in each of these different things was not just the result of idle curiosity. Viticulture or matches, clocks or writing machines, Jefferson applied himself as totally and as productively to these enterprises as he would, just half an hour later, to weighty affairs of state.

Food, and how it is grown, made and cooked, was a subject that greatly interested Jefferson. When he was in Paris from 1784 to 1789, he was constantly observing different European crops and plants and kinds of food. Pasta certainly came under this scrutiny, as is shown by his meticulous notes on how macaroni is made. Whether because of a fascination with the methods of production, or a love of the end product, Jefferson decided that he wanted one of these machines, and on 22 January 1789 he wrote from Paris to his friend William Short, then in Italy, asking him to buy him one when in Naples. On 11 February Short answered, 'I procured at Naples according to your request the mold for making maccaroni.' We can then follow the stately progress of this strange machine over the next seven months, as it goes from Naples via Marseilles to Paris. Short is in Marseilles on 3 April when he writes to Jefferson, 'I left the maccaroni machine with my banker to be sent on here to Mr Catalan but it has not yet arrived, occasioned by the contrary winds which have been reigning now near two months.' In fact it was four months later in August, when a postscript to a letter from Catalan in Marseilles

to Jefferson reads, 'I have lately received a box for you from Naples with a machine for maccarony, will you have it to Paris?' At the end of that month Jefferson answers requesting that the machine be sent to Short in Paris 'by such sure conveyance by land as shall be cheapest.' This, ten days later, Catalan replies that he will do.

At this point this unexpected little backwater of history dries up. Did the macaroni machine safely reach the shores of America? Was it installed in the kitchens of Monticello, to be brought into use when Jefferson wanted a reminder of his days in Europe? We cannot be sure. It may well have returned to the States with Jefferson, who sailed from Le Havre in October 1789 and arrived back in Norfolk, Virginia, after a near-record crossing of twenty-six days. What we do know is that one of the eighty-six crates that contained Jefferson's household effects – crate number 40, in fact – held a precious cargo: 'two cases of maccaroni.'

How the *mangiamaccheroni* went west

Jefferson's two cases of macaroni were but the precursors of countless thousands upon thousands of cases, boxes and packets of pasta that were to travel across the Atlantic about 100 years later. During the early part of the nineteenth century, however, pasta remained – outside Italy – an occasional exotic dish, often added to rather elaborate menus to give variety.

Such an occasion *par excellence* was the banquet given by the Prince Regent, later King George IV, at the Royal Pavilion, Brighton, on 15 January 1817. On this occasion, the renowned French chef Carême was in charge of the preparation of a feast which started off with four soups, followed by four kinds of fish, followed – as it built up to its grand climax – by four *pieces de résistance* (as they were known) that were surrounded by no less than thirty-six entrées. Here pasta made its modest appearance, one of these entrées being *La Timbale de Macaroni à la Napolitaine*. This was macaroni and grated cheese, layered with forcemeat, steamed in a large mould.

In the United States, up to 1880 there was a small but steady flow of immigrants from Italy. We get an idea of the conditions in which many of them lived from the writings of Charles Loring Brace, who worked very hard to help poor immigrants in New York. In 1872 he wrote: 'In the same room I would find monkeys, children, men and women, with organs and plastercasts all huddled together; but the women contriving still, in the crowded rooms, to roll their macaroni and talk excitedly.'

The years between 1880 and 1920 saw the great emigration of Italians. In just four decades, more than four million Italians emigrated to America, nearly three million of them going between 1900 and 1914. They were mostly from the South, and in 1907 almost a quarter of a million came from the Naples area alone. The story has often been told of how the agents of the steamship lines swarmed over southern Italy, painting an alluring picture of high wages and a secure future. To reach this promised land, families endured atrocious conditions of overcrowding on board ship, sometimes crammed in tiers three deep.

The start of the First World War in Europe had a dramatic effect on the flow of immigrants from Italy. The great wave of 1914, when no fewer than 283,738 Italians arrived in America, was suddenly checked, and in 1915 the figure dropped to just below 50,000. By 1919 the flow had become a trickle, with fewer than 2,000 Italians arriving. Then, the war over, the numbers surged again for one year, 1920, before two immigration acts – the first in 1921 – brought the massive movement of the previous forty years to an almost complete stop. The second act, in 1924, restricted the annual number of immigrants from any country to 2 per cent of the number of its citizens who were already resident in the United States in 1890; this curb struck particularly hard at would-be emigrants from Italy, since by 1890 only about 350,000 Italians had settled in America.

Made in America

It is not hard to imagine what a joy a plate of pasta must have been to these hard-pressed people. They were newly arrived in a strange country, often desperately poor, so a dish of spaghetti was one of their only links with the life they had left behind. Small wonder that they had no intention of abandoning the food that had been such an essential part of their old way of life, and small wonder that – as a result – imports of pasta from Italy grew to huge proportions. By 1914 imports had reached 77,000,000 pounds. Then the war brought a sharp and sudden drop in the imports of pasta – down to 30,000 pounds in 1919.

This gave an immediate boost to domestic manufacture. Already a host of back-room factories were starting up, and these rapidly increased in number. Small family enterprises, using basic and very primitive machinery to knead and extrude the pasta, found a ready market among their neighbours, who in all probability were from the same town or village in Italy. Only very slowly, through the 1920s, did the manufacture of pasta begin to catch up with the times. Families gradually began to come together to buy better machinery and manufacture in greater volume, so that they could sell to shops that were farther afield than the corner of the block.

Throughout the 1930s the pasta industry expanded steadily. Larger manufacturers began to emerge, and to build their names through advertising. Pasta was becoming part of the American way of life.

The recent history of pasta in Italy

In Italy pasta has always been an important issue, so much so that in 1926 it became a political issue. Apparently Mussolini was planning to prohibit the eating of pasta. It was known that Mussolini wanted to cast aside much that was traditional in Italy, and the story was widely believed. It took party officials all their powers of persuasion to convince the frightened populace that it was a rumour without foundation.

Before long, however, another incident caused alarm and despondency. The poet Marinetti was the founder of the Futurist movement, as well as being an ardent Fascist and a persuasive orator. In 1931 Marinetti launched an all-out attack on what he called 'the absurd Italian gastronomic religion'. 'It is necessary once and for all,' he stormed 'to annihilate pasta. It is something that is steeped in the past, a symbol of oppressive dullness, plodding deliberation and fat-bellied conceit.' The shock waves resulting from this pronouncement were felt even in America, where the National Macaroni Manufacturers' Association actually sent a telegram of protest to Mussolini. In Italy, however, everybody went on eating pasta, happily ignoring Marinetti and his campaign.

But the city of Naples was soon no longer the pasta city supremo. As thousands upon thousands of acres of land were newly planted with wheat, in order to make Italy self-sufficient, the number of grain ships unloading in the bay of Naples steadily diminished. With temperature-controlled drying tunnels replacing the hot winds from Vesuvius, and with durum wheat being grown in central and northern Italy, there was every reason to build pasta factories nearer the big centres of population in the north. By the 1940s the northern regions were beginning to produce as much pasta as the area around Naples, and since then the relative position of Naples has steadily declined. However, though Naples can no longer claim to produce the most, she still claims to produce the best.

Whether dried pasta comes from the north or the south of Italy, the probability is that it will be of really good quality. One of the reasons for this is Law No. 580. This law, which came into effect on 4 July 1967, laid down that all dried pasta sold in Italy must be made from durum semolina.

Today pasta is made in many countries of the world, and there is a thriving international trade in the manufactured product, as well as in the durum grain from which it is made. As might be expected, Italy is by far the largest producer and exporter of pasta.

Above: Pedestrians on Broadway look through a restaurant window to watch a cook prepare a pot of spaghetti. New York City, 1937.

Who eats all the pasta?

Italy leads the world in pasta consumption. In 2012 the Italians ate 26kg per capita, compared to 8.8kg in the USA and a mere 2.5kg in the UK, which was among the lowest consumption in Europe. After the Italians, the people who eat most pasta are the Venezuelans, who managed to go through some 13.2kg per person. So the British have a long way to go to catch up. I was extremely surprised by these data, since it seemed to me that most English children eat pasta for their supper, being the most welcome food and the easiest and quickest way for their busy mothers to fill them up.

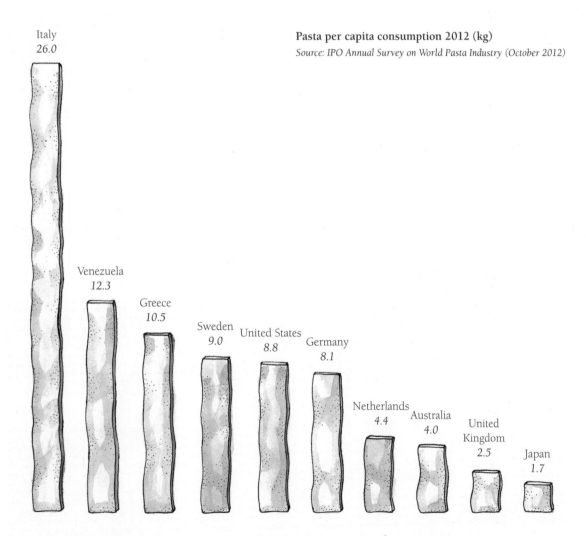

Pasta per capita consumption 2012 (kg)
Source: IPO Annual Survey on World Pasta Industry (October 2012)

Italy
26.0

Venezuela
12.3

Greece
10.5

Sweden
9.0

United States
8.8

Germany
8.1

Netherlands
4.4

Australia
4.0

United
Kingdom
2.5

Japan
1.7

Opposite: Spaghetti factory, 1932.

Pasta's many names

Pasta has not always been known as pasta. Over the centuries it has had a succession of different generic names, in a way no other food has. Bread, after all, comes in many shapes and sizes, but the basic stuff is and always has been called bread.
Correctly pasta is called **pasta alimentare** *in Italian, partly because pasta means dough in general; there is* **pasta frolla** (*sweet pastry*), **pasta sfoglia** (*puff pastry*), **pasta da pane** (*bread dough*) *and so on.*

String and little worms

It is not surprising that, until their unification, the many states, dukedoms and principalities of the Italian peninsula spoke different versions of the Italian language. Some of the different words for pasta, therefore, were local names. The word *trii* – the Arabic for string – was a name for pasta used in Palermo in the twelfth century, and still survives in parts of Sicily. Another very early reference dates from 1279, when one of the things Ponzio Bastone left his family in his will was a basketful of *macaronis*. And only a couple of decades later Marco Polo wrote about *lasagne*. Then in the *Decameron*, which Boccaccio wrote in 1350, we are back to *macaroni*.

In the fifteenth century *fidelini* was much used. This word is of Spanish origin, and is closely linked to *fideos*, which is still the word for pasta in Spain and all over Latin America.

Between about 1500 and 1800, however, there was one name for pasta in fairly general use throughout Italy and this was *vermicelli*. It is noteworthy that when John Florio wrote the first English-Italian dictionary in 1598, with the splendid title *A Worlde of Wordes or most Copious and Exact Dictionarie in Italian and English*, the two names for pasta that were included were *macaroni* and *vermicelli*. *Vermicelli* was defined by Florio as 'a kinde of paste meate like little worms.' Florio, by the way, was the man Shakespeare turned to for advice

Opposite: The Italian Market, *by Jean Mieg (1791–1862).*

about things Italian. He was the son of Protestant Italians who came to England as religious émigrés.

Until the late eighteenth century, vermicelli was the more commonly used word for pasta. But by 1800, the word was macaroni, or *maccheroni*, and so it was to remain for over a century.

The many meanings of macaroni

Macaroni turned out to be a very versatile word, going far beyond its meaning as a plate of food.

Already in Elizabethan times, those who wanted to cut a figure and to be seen as fashionable would imitate Italian ways. In Ben Jonson's play *Cynthia's Revels*, first performed in 1599, there is a superbly described character called Amorphus, who is 'a traveller. One so made out of the mixture of the shreds of forms, that himself is truly deform'd. He walks most commonly with a clove or pick-tooth in his mouth ... he speaks all cream skimm'd, and more affected than a dozen waiting women.' Amorphus had a companion, called Asotus: 'The other gallant is his zany, and doth most of his tricks after him. He doth learn to make strange sauces, to eat anchovies, maccaroni, bovoli [a kind of cockle], fagioli and caviar, because *he* loves them.' If you liked odd food and ate macaroni, you did so in order to tell the world that you were a 'traveller', and that having been as far as Italy, you were well above the common people.

Others, of course, might put a different interpretation on it, and by the eighteenth century, when many more Englishmen – and a scattering of women – went to Europe, those who affected Italian habits came in for a considerable amount of mockery. This scathing comment appeared in the *Oxford Magazine* in 1770: 'There is indeed a kind of animal, neither male nor female, a thing of the neuter gender, lately started up amongst us. It is called a Macaroni. It talks without meaning, it smiles without pleasantry, it eats without appetite, it rides without exercise, it wenches without passion.' This description seems to be inspired by a scorn of things foreign, but the macaronies themselves were proud of their Italian connection. Around 1760, they had formed the Macaroni Club, to which Horace Walpole refers in a letter: 'The Macaroni Club is composed of all the travelled young men who wear long curls and spying glasses.'

For about 100 years in England, between 1750 and 1850, a macaroni was not a dish of pasta but any affected, overdressed person – in short, a dandy. But the particular affectation of those eighteenth-century macaronies that most caught the public fancy, and came in for the most abuse, was the wearing of fantastic wigs with the hair piled high in truly amazing style. It is those hairstyles that gave a species of penguins with an orange-coloured crest (*Eudyptes chrysolophus*) the English name of macaroni penguin.

Sometimes it was the coiffure, rather than the person, that was called a macaroni. And that is why, when Yankee Doodle came to town upon a little pony and stuck a feather in his hat, he called it macaroni. If he sounds a bit daft – and 'doodle' indeed meant someone who could be so described – this is because the song was first sung by the British to make fun of the Yankees. Then, when the colonial troops routed the British at Lexington, they sang 'Yankee Doodle' mockingly at the British and claimed the song as their own.

Finally, there is one further addition to the number of words and meanings that grew from the eighteenth-century travellers' fondness for showing off their foreign habits. An early nineteenth-century Dictionary of the Turf defines the Macaroni Stakes as 'those ridden by gentlemen, not jockeys.' Ridiculous they may have been, dandies they certainly were, but jockeys ... never!

Back in Italy, the story of the word macaroni in all its meanings leads us to Mantua in the early sixteenth century, and a man called Teofilo Folengo, who has been described as 'an occasional monk.' He did indeed become a Benedictine monk, but when he was only twenty-five he found the bonds of monastic life too oppressive, and left to travel the country. But ten ears later Folengo was safely back in his monastery, turning his literary skills to advantage with an account of his wanderings. He wrote under the pen name of Merlin Coccai, and his best-known work was the poem 'Baldus' – a comic, and highly unmonastic, parody of the poems of chivalry. However, what earned him the most fame, and a place in this story, was the language in which he wrote 'Baldus' and other works. This was a cross between Latin and Italian, made up mostly of Italian words with Latin endings. The resulting mixture, which was designed to make the racy Italian sound like monkish Latin, was called by Folengo *poesia maccheronica* – macaronic poetry. It was, he said, a literary equivalent of macaroni, which he described as 'a gross, rude and rustic mixture of flour, cheese and butter.' And the term is still used to describe verse in a jumbled mixture of vernacular and Latin (or Latin-sounding) words.

Opposite: The Grub Street Macaroni (*engraving*), *English School*, (*18th century*).

THE GRUB STREET MACARONI.

Pub accor to act Feb.y 3, 1772 by MDarly Strand.

The new names

Pasta is now the generic word, and vermicelli, lasagne and maccheroni or macaroni are just three of the myriad of names to describe all the forms and shapes in which pasta can be bought. (Noodles, a widely used term in American English, derives from the German word *Nudel*.) The ribbons of pasta known as tagliatelle take their name from the word *tagliare*, which means 'to cut'. These days tagliatelle are more narrowly defined as between 6 and 8mm wide. Other names describe the shapes of the pasta, from the tiny *orzo* (like grains of barley), to *conchiglie* (shells) in various sizes, and *penne* (quill pens).

In Italy the word *pasta* has been in general use since the 1930s. However, regionalism lingers on in Italy, and certain kinds of pasta are local specialities with local names. When in Genoa you should ask for *trenette*, in Venice for *bigoli*, in Sardinia for *malloreddus*, and when you are next in Naples you will make a deep impression on the locals if you ask for *strangulaprievete*, and in Puglia for *cavatiedde*.

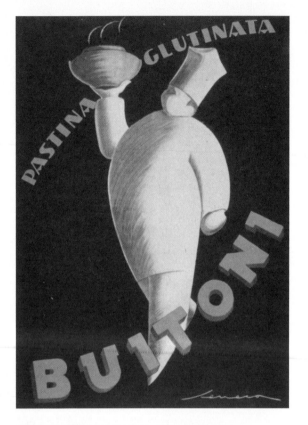

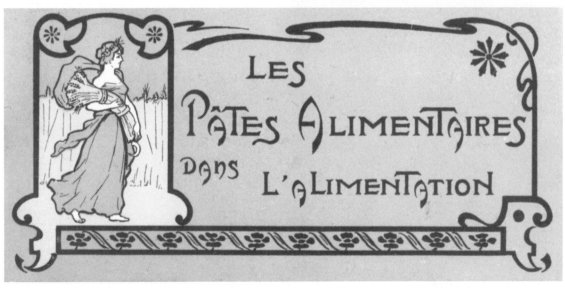

Above and opposite: Early twentieth-century French and Italian advertising designs. Paste Alimentari is the term for pasta in Italian.

PASTE
ALIMENTARI

MARCA
REGISTRATA

PASTIFICIO
TRIESTINO
SOCIETA ANONIMA
TRIESTE

Creazione: S. POLLIONE

Pasta people

A lover, a dramatist, two poets, two composers, two singers, a mayor, a novelist and a film star,
a model and a tennis champion. All of these famous people have spoken on the subject of pasta.

The lover

Casanova needs no introduction. At the age of eighteen, not long after he was expelled from a seminary in Venice for immoral conduct, he stayed briefly at nearby Chioggia, where it is recorded that he looked so noble, and ate so much pasta, that he was dubbed 'the macaroni prince'. To mark the occasion Casanova allegedly recited a sonnet in honour of macaroni, but sadly this has not survived. It is nonetheless interesting that macaroni should have been one of the early loves of so famous a lover.

The playwright

Only a few years before Casanova was removed from his seminary, Carlo Goldoni was also a young student in Venice – but of a much more serious kind. However, one summer, he and a friend met up with a company of travelling actors on a riverboat. Years afterwards, Goldoni recounted in his memoirs how they spent a happy afternoon playing cards with the actors, and 'Then the supper bell rang, and we all rushed to eat. Macaroni! Everyone fell on it, three bowlfuls were devoured; beef, cold chicken, veal, fruit, delicious wine: what a meal! what appetites!'

The English poet

Venice seems to forge a link between pasta and amorous activities. Several decades after Casanova's career was in full swing, we find Lord Byron spending a few hectic years there, during which time he wrote Canto II of *Don Juan*. This contains a verse which suggests that pasta has hitherto unsuspected aphrodisiac qualities:

Ceres presents a plate of vermicelli,
For love must be sustained like flesh and blood,
While Bacchus pours out wine, or hands a jelly:
Eggs, oysters, too, are amatory food.

The French poet

Alfred de Musset described Naples as that blessed land '...*où sont nés les macaroni et la musique*' – 'where macaroni and music were born.'

The first composer

Many of Rossini's happiest compositions were culinary ones, for he was a cook of some distinction. He loved food, and of all foods he loved pasta best. There are several stories about Rossini and pasta, and various references to it in his letters. He wrote a letter, for instance, from Paris to a friend in Naples, the main burden of which was a lament that the macaroni he had asked to be sent from Naples had still not arrived. He signed himself 'G. Rossini, *senza maccheroni*!!'

In 1815, the impresario Domenico Barbaia invited Rossini to his palace in Naples for six months, and there bestowed lavish hospitality on him, on the understanding that in return Rossini would compose a new opera, *Otello*. There followed six highly enjoyable months of Neapolitan pasta, wine and women ... but no music . Not a note was written. So Barbaia locked Rossini in his room, and – the worst penalty of all ... but we shall let Rossini describe this in his own words, writing to his devoted sister: 'I have composed the overture to *Otello* in a room in Barbaia's house, where the baldest and most ferocious impresario has kept me prisoner, without any other pleasure but one dish of pasta a day, and with the threat of keeping me prisoner here until I write the finale.' However, it was Rossini who got the last laugh. He gained his release by the simple ruse of handing Barbaia four sections, marked Overture, Acts 1, 2 and 3, which – after he had gone – were found to differ only in their title pages, each merely containing the score of the overture, which Rossini had copied out four times.

An account of Rossini and pasta could not possibly end without a story that will be of great comfort to those who, like Rossini, find it hard to remember names and faces. A man sat next to him one day at dinner and said, 'You remember me, I'm sure. I met you at that dinner given in your honour, when there was a splendid macaroni pie.' Rossini thought for a long time, then slowly shook his head. 'I certainly remember the macaroni pie,' he said, 'but I'm afraid I don't remember you.'

The second composer

Verdi's feelings for pasta may not have been as passionate as Rossini's, but that is not to say he was immune to its attractions. When he was staying in St Petersburg one April and sorely missing the warmth of the Italian spring, his wife wrote in a letter that 'it would take really perfect tagliatelle and macaroni to put him in a good mood, amidst all this ice and all these fur coats.'

The singers

Both Caruso and Mario Lanza are known to have been inordinately fond of pasta. Caruso, when staying at his hotel in New York City, used to give dinner parties at which he would cook the spaghetti himself, and dress it with superb sauces. And Mario Lanza once said that the one thing that really made him sing was spaghetti.

The mayor

Speaking to the United Nations about giving aid to countries in need, former New York mayor Fiorello La Guardia made the only reference to pasta that has found its way into a dictionary of quotations. 'Ticker tape,' he said 'ain't spaghetti.' In other words, you can't eat the news.

The novelist

Mario Puzo, author of *The Godfather*, once said: 'Seven days without a plate of spaghetti drops me into a deep, dark well of physical anxiety.'

The film star

Sophia Loren, when asked how American women could become as attractive as the Italians, answered: 'Everything you see I owe to spaghetti.'

The tennis champion

Maria Sharapova, in one of her post-match interviews, is quoted as saying: 'I have been very competitive by nature from an early age, whether it was eating a bowl of pasta faster than somebody else, or always wanting to be the first one in line.'

Spaghetti fictions

Pasta, in a modest way, has its own mythology. Although this is not rooted in antiquity in the same way as is that of bread, there are a number of tales and legends about a food that, in one country at least, is as important as bread.
The earliest legend tells how Ceres, goddess of agriculture and crops, spurned Vulcan, who was the Roman god of fire, and how Vulcan took his revenge by stripping every grain of wheat from the fields. He then ground the grains with his iron club, plunged them into the bay of Naples, cooked them in the flames of Vesuvius and dressed this celestial dish with oil from the olives of Capri. Thus was pasta created, by a Roman god.

The emperor and the magician

Another story set in Naples is a legend that is still very much alive in the city in slightly different versions; the fact that they all contain references to an actual emperor suggests that there may be a germ of truth in the story. The emperor in question is Frederick II, who was crowned King of Sicily in Palermo in 1198, when he was four. It must have been a very small crown.

The central character in the story, however, is not the king but a magician called Chicco. Chicco lived in one room in a house in Naples, and he spent his days shut in that room carrying out curious experiments. No one knew where he came from and no one could decide what he was doing. When asked, he would only say that all he wanted to do in life was to make mankind happy. This, coupled with his striking looks, and his air of having once been a rich man, only increased his neighbours' curiosity. The more daring among them had managed to snatch an occasional glimpse into his room, and they swore that he was cooking something in a vast cauldron. Magic potions, perhaps? Or could it have been something far more sinister? Imagine, if you can, the excitement in the neighbourhood when he was heard to cry out that he had discovered what all his life he had been seeking.

Now it so happened that the most curious and the most suspicious of his neighbours was a certain Giovannella, a lady of unsympathetic character who is in fact the villain of this tale. Giovannella was so curious that she used to spend her days spying on Chicco by looking through his keyhole, with the result that she – and she alone – had a very good idea of just what he *was* doing. It also so happened that Giovannella's husband was a cook at the court of Frederick II, who was now the Holy Roman Emperor. When Chicco made his discovery, Giovannella saw that her moment had come. She persuaded her husband that they could become rich by selling Chicco's secret, and pressed him to approach the Emperor. This he did, and Frederick agreed that his cook's wife should come to the palace and make this mysterious new dish for him. So Giovannella was sent for, and the servants in the kitchen were ordered to provide her with everything she needed. But all she asked for was flour and water!

The story goes on to tell how she made marvellous macaroni with a delicious sauce, and how this was presented to the Emperor, who was so delighted with the new dish that he ordered her to come to him. When he asked her how she had discovered this superb new food, Giovannella answered that it was by divine revelation. Then the Emperor sent his chef to learn from her, and he paid her a great deal of money for her secret. And after that all the nobles and dignitaries at court paid her money, and then the merchants, and then even those who could ill afford the price she asked for her recipe. Giovannella, on the other hand, was becoming richer and richer.

Of course, it was not very long before Chicco chanced on someone cooking the new dish, and when he asked who had discovered it he was told an angel had revealed the secret to a Neapolitan woman. So appalled was he on hearing this that he felt he could not stay in Naples another day. Before night had fallen Chicco had left Naples forever, and no one knew where he had gone. What most people said, however, was that he had been taken away by the Devil.

The years passed by, and Giovannella lived on, rich and seemingly happy, until one day she fell terribly ill. Then, as her illness grew worse and she lay dying, she confessed all she had done and appealed to God for forgiveness and mercy. Two days later, on a Saturday, she died. And ever since that day, Chicco has come back to the house every Saturday night. Then he is to be seen making his pasta, while Giovannella ceaselessly stirs the sauce, and all the while the Devil blows on the fire to keep it hot.

Miraculous macaroni

In 1537 Pope Paul III beatified Guglielmo Cuffitella, who had lived his holy life in Sicily more than 100 years earlier. He thus became *il Beato Guglielmo*: the Blessed William. The process of beatification calls for evidence that two miracles have been brought about by the person concerned, and in a twelve-volume book called *The Acts of the Saints*, published in 1675, we read that Guglielmo's two qualifying miracles were both performed in connection with a plate of pasta! Both miracles also feature a certain Guiccione, who was the blessed one's particular friend, and Guiccione's wife, who was a singularly disagreeable woman.

Miracle the first: One day Guiccione invited the holy man to supper, having asked his wife to make ravioli. This she did, but with a difference, since to spite her saintly guest she gave him ravioli that she had stuffed with husks instead of meat. Guglielmo was not slow to notice what was up, but taking this in his stride, he made the sign of the Cross over the offending plate, opened a few of the ravioli, and exclaimed, 'How delicious!' And behold! The ravioli were filled, not with husks, but with ricotta cheese.

Miracle the second: One Ash Wednesday, Guiccione again asked his holy friend to supper. But this time Guglielmo, knowing the difficulties that might result, said that he could not come because he was expecting a visitor. Whereupon the kindly Guiccione sent his little boy over with a dish of steaming hot lasagne. Guiccione's wicked wife seemed to offer no objection to this, but as she gave the boy the dish she whispered in his ear not to give the dish to Guglielmo, but instead to hide it in his cupboard. The days of Lent passed by, and Guiccione was more and more puzzled to receive neither his empty dish back, nor any thanks. In the end he sent the boy to Guglielmo's house, where the boy went straight to the cupboard where he had hidden the lasagne. He opened it, and there was the dish, piled high with the same lasagne – and it was steaming as if it had just been taken from the pot. 'But, don't you remember?' said Guglielmo to the amazed boy, 'you brought me the lasagne just now.'

No pasta

'...and the day dawned on which all Italy sat down to dinner without pasta.' This awful eventuality comes to pass in *Italian Peepshow* by Eleanor Farjeon, a charming book of children's stories about Italy first published in the 1920s. There was no pasta because the crop had failed that year, and the young reader is left in no doubt as to the gravity of the disaster. Earlier in the story it had been explained that 'Pasta is important to Italians' and this solemn statement is followed by a list of the different shapes of pasta:

> *Shells and*
> *Bells and*
> *Nuts and*
> *Apple-pips and*
> *Needle-points and*
> *Fleas' Eyes and*
> *Horses' Teeth and*
> *Holy Seeds and*
> *Olive Stones and*
> *Linen Sheets and*
> *Hearts and*
> *Diamonds and*
> *Feathers and*
> *The Virgin's Tears*

When that awful day dawned on which there was no pasta, such a wail went up that it was heard across the sea by King Nero of Tripoli. At first he could not think what the noise might be, but fearing that it was the crying of men and children, he set sail and followed the cry across the sea to Italy. There, when he asked them, 'For what do you cry?', they answered, 'For pasta' and although one little golden-haired child ran away at the sight of his dusky face, he promised to try and bring them their pasta.

So he went to the sea shore and asked the sea for its shells, and the sea said, 'With pleasure, if the church will give you its bells,' and so the king asked his way right through the list until he came to the Virgin's tears. But the Virgin said she needed her tears to weep with. 'The earth is angry with the fair child,' she said, 'and refuses to bear corn in her country until of her own free will the child kisses a black man.' Then the King asked the Virgin for her tears so that he could weep in her place, and she gave them to him, and all the others then gave him what he asked for: the church its bells, the sea its shells and so on and so forth.

Then King Nero drove his golden chariot through Italy, scattering bells and shells and apple-pips wherever he went, and as they fell to the ground they all turned to pasta. At last he reached the village where the golden-haired girl lived, and as he entered the market square she ran out and gave him a kiss. At this the King beamed with happiness, and at the same moment the earth once again began to grow its crop.

Opposite: Gathering the spaghetti harvest in Ticino, Switerland. A still from a spoof TV documentary first shown in the UK on 1 April 1957, by the BBC.

Full of goodness

'One of the least fattening cuisines in the world is the Italian cuisine: the real Italian cuisine consisting of a plate of pasta with tomato sauce, dressed with a little grated Parmesan, followed by a little meat or fish, a salad and fresh fruit.'
Ancel Keys (1904–2004), Professor Emeritus of Physiological Hygiene, University of Minnesota

Most people love pasta. It is delicious and it is filling, and that is what we all want our food to be. It is also healthy, since it contains very little fat and quite a high amount of carbohydrate, which gives us energy.

Pasta is among the most easily digestible foods there is. Not only is it very easily digested, it is also very rapidly assimilated, as it is quickly converted by the digestive processes into glucose. In this form it acts as a fuel for the body and provides abundant energy.

A dish of pasta is widely recommended to athletes and sportsmen or women before a competition.

Since pasta is always eaten with other ingredients, it provides a varied and valuable source of nutrition. One day you eat it with tomatoes and/or other vegetables, another day with cheese, another day with meat, and another with fish. All the different foods you need join with pasta to make the basis of a meal that is easily digested, nourishing and healthy.

Buying pasta

Pasta can of course be bought at any supermarket, but if you are within reach of an Italian deli you will find a far greater variety of shapes there, and probably some of the best-quality Italian pasta. It is worth going out of your way to buy good pasta, as the difference in taste is quite considerable, and the difference in price is small.

The main thing to look for when buying dried pasta is that it must state on the package that it is made from durum wheat (or durum semolina). This is quite essential, as pasta made wholly or partly from bread wheat tastes less good and goes mushy when cooked.

Apart from what it says on the packet, you can tell a lot about the quality of pasta by looking at the raw pasta itself: it should be a pale buff yellow colour, rather than grey. When held up to the light, pasta should be translucent – though you cannot see through the double thickness of hollow shapes – with dark specs visible within it.

After cooking properly, in plenty of boiling water and for the right amount of time (see 'The five golden rules for cooking pasta' on page 56, or 'A different method of cooking dried pasta' on page 57), good-quality pasta will look moist, with every piece well separated – and it should have at least doubled in volume. Good-quality pasta has a taste of its own, which I would call delicate, not bland.

Shapes

I never counted how many different shapes of pasta there are in an Italian supermarket, although I have read that there are more than 300 shapes. Having said that, I must add that some shapes are given different names by different manufacturers: *mafalde*, for instance, are also called *reginette*; vermicelli are also known as *fidelini* or spaghettini. To simplify matters, what I suggest you do is to have four or five different shapes in your cupboard (two long, two short and one small, let's say). And maybe a packet of dried egg lasagne and one of tagliatelle might come in handy.

With each recipe I have indicated the shape or shapes of pasta that are best suited to that particular sauce. If you want to use another shape – because you cannot find the one listed, or because you have already a similar shape in your cupboard, or just for a change – the principle to remember is that long pasta goes better with oil-based sauces, such as tomato or fish sauces, while short pasta is best for a heavy, meaty sauce. This is because the short varieties are either convoluted in shape, grooved or hollow, so that they pick up more of the sauce and thus give the dish a richer taste. So it is usually best to substitute one type of long pasta for another, or one type of short pasta for another. However, this is not to be taken as a rigid rule, since – for example – an excellent dish of pasta with ragú can be made with penne or tagliatelle.

Long pasta

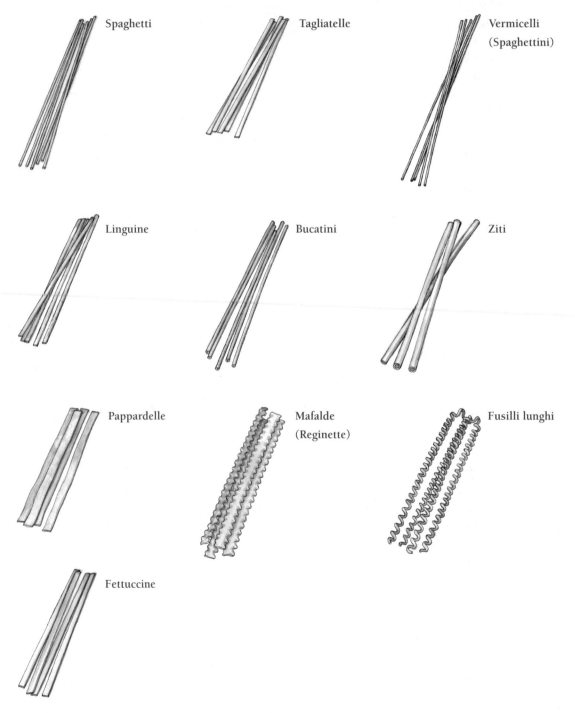

Spaghetti

Tagliatelle

Vermicelli
(Spaghettini)

Linguine

Bucatini

Ziti

Pappardelle

Mafalde
(Reginette)

Fusilli lunghi

Fettuccine

Small pasta

{ Pastina }

Orzo

Quadretti

Alfabeto

Stelline

Ditalini

Short pasta

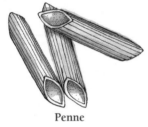

Penne

Maccheroni

Sedani

Fusilli

Ruote

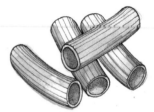

Rigatoni

Tortiglioni

Trofie

Ditali

Conchiglie

Orecchiette

Gomiti

Garganelli

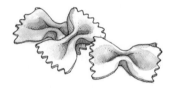

Farfalle

Gnocchetti sardi

Spirali

Stuffed pasta

Agnolotti

This is the traditional stuffed pasta from Piedmont, where there are as many different stuffings as there are cooks. Agnolotti used to be made on Mondays with the leftover meat from Sunday – roasted, braised or boiled. They also often contain spinach or cabbage, and during the autumn they are sometimes enriched with white truffle. There are also agnolotti from Tuscany, which include calves' brains in the stuffing.

Anolini

One of the many stuffed shapes from Emilia-Romagna. Traditionally they are stuffed with meat and served *in brodo* – 'in stock' – as a soup. See recipe on page 192.

Cannelloni

Made in a few regions of Italy with different stuffings, cannelloni originated in Piedmont, where traditionally they are made with pancakes. However, they are also made with pasta and stuffed with meat (see recipe on page 191). In Naples they are stuffed with prosciutto, mozzarella and ricotta, while in Rome they often contain lambs' brains and sausage.

Cappellacci

A speciality of Ferrara (Romagna), cappellacci are large cappelletti or ravioli containing a purée of local pumpkin, breadcrumbs, Parmesan, egg and nutmeg. They are dressed with melted butter and grated Parmesan.

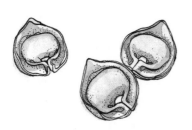

Cappelletti

A classic shape of Romagna, the eastern part of Emilia-Romagna, the traditional cappelletti have a stuffing of pork, chicken, prosciutto, Parmesan and spices (or of minced capon, ricotta, spices and Parmesan), and are served *in brodo*, which in this case should be a capon stock. If served *asciutti* – not in stock, but drained – they are always dressed simply with butter and/or cream and Parmesan, or a very light tomato sauce.

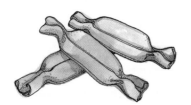

Caramelle

This modern stuffed pasta takes its name from the sweets wrapped in paper. The stuffing varies widely; it is often vegetarian, like potato, sometimes mixed with celeriac, or aubergine and ricotta. They are mostly dressed with butter and cheese or a light tomato sauce.

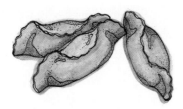

Casonsei or casoncelli

This is the traditional horseshoe-shaped stuffed pasta from eastern Lombardy. Besides the usual filling of Parmesan, salame and sausage, it may also contain pear or amaretti, raisins or spinach. It sounds odd, but good casonsei are superb. They are usually dressed with melted butter, sage and Parmesan.

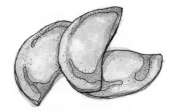

Cjalsons or cialzons

Hailing from Friuli, cjalsons are stuffed with potatoes and chives (a popular herb in the region) or spinach, to which sweet ingredients are added, such as grated chocolate or cocoa powder, sultanas, cinnamon and crumbled biscuits. They are dressed with butter and smoked ricotta, a speciality of Carnia in Friuli.

Pansooti, pansôti

These are the stuffed pasta of Liguria. They are stuffed with '*preboggion*', which is a mixture of fresh local wild herbs (borage, parsley, chicory, mint, sage and others), plus ricotta, eggs and Parmesan. They are traditionally dressed with salsa di noci – walnut sauce (page 147).

Ravioli, raviolini, ravioloni

Different size parcels, either square or round, with different stuffings, made all over Italy, but especially in the North. There are many variations, from the usual meat stuffing (page 188), to all sorts of vegetable stuffings (spinach and ricotta, aubergine and mozzarella), fish and seafood. The ravioli of Puglia, usually round, are stuffed with a purée of chickpeas seasoned with sugar and a touch of grated chocolate and then dressed with olive oil and, when in season, raw local mushrooms. Ravioloni. a modern shape, are very large ravioli, sometimes 15cm/6 inches square, which are served singly, either in stock or on a vegetable purée.

Tortelli, tortelloni

These are the ravioli of Lombardy and are always vegetarian. In northern Lombardy the stuffing is potato or spinach (the local crops) with ricotta, Parmesan and eggs. In the southern part of the region the traditional tortelli are filled with pumpkin plus crumbled amaretti, ricotta, eggs and sometimes chopped mostarda di Cremona, the spicy local fruit relish, one of the glories of the town of Cremona – after the Stradivarius violins.

Tortellini

The stuffed pasta of Bologna par excellence; there are two legends attached to their origins. The first one tells of an innkeeper who, having spied through the keyhole of a bedroom a beautiful maiden lying naked, became so excited by her navel that he had to rush into the kitchen and reproduce it with the pasta dough that was waiting to be used. In the other legend it was the goddess Venus who was spied naked by the innkeeper. Tortellini do look like belly buttons and the recipe on page 194 tells you how to make them. Tortellini are usually stuffed with meat and served *in brodo*, in a delicate chicken stock, like a soup.

Eating pasta

The rest of the meal

Any meal must have a good balance of different kinds of food.

Pasta can be a first course, as it generally is in Italy, or a main – and only – course. This 'one-course meal' has become very popular nowadays. The English and the Americans were, in fact, the first people to eat pasta as a single course, often accompanied by a salad. This combination is not at all Italian. In Italy the salad would never be eaten with the pasta, but after.

If you serve pasta as a first course, the rest of the meal should be light and different from the sauce of the pasta, although not strongly contrasting with it. Let me give you an example. After a steaming bowl of bucatini alla carbonara (page 86), a dish of mixed roast vegetables or some fillets of sole braised in wine would be perfect, as would a few slices of prosciutto or ham and salad.

Many of the dishes described in this book make a complete meal in themselves – for example, all the baked pasta dishes, as well as others such as the farfalle with kidneys (page 91) or the ziti with haddock fillets (page 109). These rich dishes should be followed only by a green salad or some sautéed courgettes or spinach with oil and garlic.

It is very difficult to give hard and fast rules, since what you want to eat is up to you alone. It also depends on the occasion. A light supper could consist only of spaghetti with leeks (page 149), but this would hardly be ideal for a Sunday lunch, when everybody expects a roast. But cannelloni stuffed with meat (page 191) or maccheroncini with pheasant sauce (page 102) might be a perfect alternative.

What to drink with pasta

There are those who say that to drink anything other than water with pasta is profanity; others swear by beer. While I cannot subscribe to the water theory, there is no doubt that beer is a good accompaniment to pasta in most of its many guises. However, I think wine is the perfect match for pasta – they might have been made for each other.

On the question of red or white, it is impossible to be dogmatic. It all depends on the sauce, of course, and there are a few sauces that demand one or the other. But on the whole pasta is very tolerant, and either red or white wine can be drunk with most of the sauces in this book with equal pleasure. There follows a simple list of those sauces whose taste definitely goes best with one or the other. The best way to take it from there is to experiment and to be guided by your own palate. The worst that can happen, after all, is that you will have the pleasure of trying again.

Recipe	Red or White wine
Tagliolini with asparagus (p.88)	White
Spaghetti with leeks (p.149)	White
Spaghetti with caviar (p.112)	White
Pasta with fresh sardines (p.172)	White
Trenette with pesto (p.138)	White
Farfalle with kidneys (p.91)	Red
Maccheroncini with pheasant sauce (p.102)	Red
Linguine with 'nduja (p.93)	Red
Stuffed cannelloni (p.191)	Red
Pappardelle with hare (p.95)	Red
Bucatini with pancetta (p.97)	Red
Macaroni with lamb *ragú* (p.98)	Red

Cooking perfect pasta

Buy only pasta made from durum wheat.
Use a large saucepan, preferably deep and cylindrical.
Make sure that the water is boiling and salted when you drop in the pasta.
Do not leave the kitchen while the pasta is cooking.
Do not overdrain pasta; it should be dripping with water.
Use good ingredients for the sauce.
Taste the sauce often.

How much pasta to use

If you are serving pasta as the first course, 85g/3oz per person is about right. For the main course this should be increased to about 100–125g/4oz per person.

Most of the recipes in this book are for 4 people. This is stated in each case.

The five golden rules for cooking dried pasta

It is not difficult to cook pasta well, but it does require some care. *Gli spaghetti amano la compagnia* – spaghetti loves company! Never leave the kitchen while the pasta is cooking: it can't take care of itself. The timing is crucial, and just 2 minutes more or less can spoil a dish that in every other way is perfect. The best way to test whether the pasta is cooked is to take some out and have a bite.

For cooking homemade pasta, see page 62.

1_Use a large saucepan in which to boil the water. The best shape is a deep cylinder, which allows the water to come back to the boil quickly after the pasta is added and keep boiling fast, which is essential for achieving a good result.

The proportion of water to pasta is:

1 litre/1¾ pints/4 cups water to 100g/3½oz pasta

2_ The salt, which should be coarse sea salt, must be added to the water at least 30 seconds before the pasta is added to allow it to dissolve.

The recommended quantity of salt is 10g/2 tsp per litre of water. If that sounds a lot, do not forget that the pasta is drained from the salted water; in Italy we say that the water should be as salty as the Mediterranean, not the Atlantic! If you want a plate of pasta worth eating, please add at least 1 teaspoon of salt for each litre of water. The salt in the sauce is not enough and does not penetrate the pasta.

3_The water must be boiling rapidly *before* the pasta is dropped into it. Add all the pasta at once, and stir with a wooden spoon to prevent it from sticking. If you are cooking long pasta, ease it in as rapidly as you can without breaking it. Then stir it to separate the strands. Cover the pan to bring the water back to the boil as quickly as possible, and remove the lid as soon as it does. Stir again, and then adjust the heat so that the water boils fast without boiling over. Some cooks add 1 teaspoon of olive oil to the water before the pasta is added to prevent it from sticking. This is never done in Italy, and I have never found it necessary.

4_ The cooking time varies according to the quality, size and shape of the pasta. If the pasta is going to be served immediately, it should be al dente: this means firm to the bite. You can follow the instructions on the packet, but taste the pasta a minute before the given time, in case you prefer it more al dente. If you like it rather soft, leave it for a little longer, but no more than 30 seconds. Drain it as soon as it reaches this point, as it will continue to cook until it is drained.

If the pasta is going to be baked, drain it when it is still just a little hard to the bite, about 2 minutes before it reaches the al dente point.

5_Have a colander ready in the sink. As soon as the pasta is cooked, pour it from the saucepan into the colander and toss briskly two or three times. If you are using pasta with a hole, drain it a bit longer than spaghetti, but *do not overdrain any pasta*.

For some recipes a cupful of the pasta cooking water should be kept to add, if necessary, to the drained pasta. This is advisable when the pasta is dressed with some creamy sauces, such as carbonara. In Naples, the motherland of good pasta, a small earthenware jug of the cooking water is usually put on the table for the diners to add to their plate.

Do not leave drained pasta standing undressed; if the sauce isn't ready, toss the pasta with a little olive oil. When dressed, *la pasta non aspetta nessuno* – pasta does not wait for anybody; it must be eaten straight away.

A different method of cooking dried pasta

When I was researching this book, I went to see Ingegner Vincenzo Agnesi, at that time the owner of the renowned pasta factory in Liguria. Agnesi described his method of cooking dried pasta. It is a method that breaks many of the established rules, and yet I have found it has several distinct advantages over the orthodox way of cooking pasta.

The startling thing about this method is that the pasta cooks for most of the time in water that has gone off the boil. The advantages are:

The pasta keeps its 'soul' (the innermost part) better. Even if you leave it in the hot water for a minute or two too long, the pasta does not become gluey – as it does if left too long in boiling water.

Because of this, there is no need to stand over the saucepan, keeping a watch and tasting the whole time. You can do something else while the pasta is cooking; if you set the timer you don't even need to stay in the kitchen.

You save gas or electricity, since after boiling the water for only 2 minutes, you turn off the heat.

The pasta retains more of the natural goodness of the wheat during the cooking process. This can be seen in the fact that the water is still clear after the pasta has been cooked in it.

Try it for yourself, following these instructions:

1_Use the same large saucepan you usually use for cooking pasta, and the usual proportions of water and salt to the quantity of pasta you want to cook. When the water is boiling rapidly, put all the pasta in at once. Stir thoroughly with a wooden spoon or a long fork.

2_Cover the saucepan to bring the water back to the boil as quickly as possible. As soon as it boils, remove the lid and boil fast for 2 minutes only.

3_Turn off the heat and stir thoroughly. Lay a thick absorbent tea towel over the saucepan, and put the lid tightly over the cloth. Wait for the same length of time given on the packet instructions for normal cooking.

4_Drain the pasta – but never too much. Pasta should still be dripping wet after it has been drained.

Homemade pasta

Pasta is made at home in most regions of Italy: in the South with durum wheat semolina and water and in the North with soft wheat flour and eggs. This is because durum wheat grows in the South, while soft wheat is the cereal of the North. Durum wheat pasta is homemade only in southern Italy. It is very difficult to make, because the dough is very unyielding and hard to stretch. I have tried many times to make orecchiette (the most common shape) but never really succeeded. So I buy dried orecchiette – far easier.

In most countries, homemade pasta means pasta made with flour and eggs. This pasta has its motherland in Emilia-Romagna, a region of fertile land and rich food. The local cooking is based on dairy products and pork, and these rich ingredients produce the ideal sauces to complement fresh egg pasta. So much importance is attributed to the ability to produce a fine sfoglia (which means the stretched-out dough) that when a girl from another region married a man from Emilia-Romagna she used to go into training with her mother-in-law to learn how to make a good sfoglia.

Fresh pasta can be bought in most supermarkets, but it is a far inferior product to pasta made at home. In fact, if you cannot make your own, I recommend buying a good brand of dried egg pasta, rather than chilled fresh pasta. Outside Italy, there is often a tendency to think that fresh pasta is better than dried pasta. There is no better or worse; they are two different products, as you cannot compare a piece of linen with a piece of silk.

Pasta all'uovo { *Homemade egg pasta* }

The idea of making pasta at home may be daunting, but once you have mastered the basic technique the process takes no more than an hour from start to finish, and the result is really worth the effort. This is the traditional Emilian way of making egg pasta, and although in other regions milk, olive oil or water are sometimes added, this recipe calls only for flour and eggs.

Use only Italian 00 flour and large eggs. It is impossible to give a hard-and-fast rule about how much flour to add to each egg because egg sizes vary, but the correct proportion is approximately 100g to each egg.

To roll out the dough the traditional Italian way, you will need a long thin rolling pin, at least 80cm/ 32 inches long, and a large smooth work surface: wood is ideal. In Italy most households used to have *l'asse per la pasta* – the board for making pasta – which measured about 1.5 x 1 metre/4 x 3 feet. It was kept standing along a wall in the kitchen and was used exclusively for making pasta.

Read through all the instructions before beginning: the process is slightly different if you are rolling by hand or using a hand-cranked machine. There are basically two types of pasta machine on the market: an electric one and a hand-cranked machine. I am not giving instructions on how to use an electric machine; just follow the manufacturer's instructions. I am here to tell you how to use the hand-cranked machine, which I strongly recommend.

For 3 to 4 people
200g/7oz/generous 1½ cups Italian 00 flour

2 eggs

a pinch of fine sea salt

For 5 to 6 people
300g/10½oz/scant 2½ cups Italian 00 flour

3 eggs

a pinch of fine sea salt

Place the flour in a mound on a clean work surface. Make a well in the centre and break the eggs into it. Add a pinch of salt. Start beating the eggs with a fork, gradually drawing the flour from the inside of the well [see Fig. 1].

When the paste thickens, mix in the rest of the flour with your hands and quickly work it until the mixture forms a mass. It will still be lumpy. If it is too sticky and moist, add a bit more flour until the mixture stops sticking to your hands. You don't necessarily need all the flour.

Set the mixture aside and thoroughly clean the work surface, using a knife to scrape off the crumbs. Then wash your hands, removing every trace of dough. Dry them well.

Lightly flour the work surface and your hands. Knead the dough with the heel of your hands, not the palm, folding it over toward you and pressing against it away from you, one hand at a time. Do this over and over again, turning it around as you work, for about 10 minutes or until the dough is elastic, smooth and compact [see Fig. 2].

Now, if you are rolling the dough by hand, you must let it rest for at least 30 minutes – or up to 3 hours. Wrap it in clingfilm and set aside.

If you have a hand-cranked pasta machine, knead the dough for only 3–5 minutes, and then proceed to roll it through the machine (see page 61).

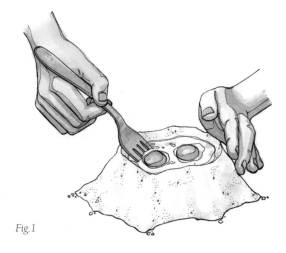

Fig.1

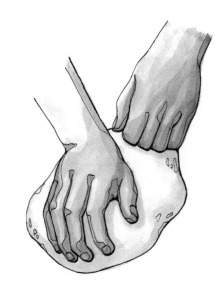

Fig.2

Rolling out by hand

If you are making the pasta with more than 2 eggs, divide the dough in half, leaving one half wrapped in clingfilm while you work on the other. Lightly flour the work surface and the rolling pin. Pat the dough into a flattish ball and begin gently rolling away from you to open out the ball. After each roll, rotate the dough so that it remains circular *[see Fig. 3]*.

Fig.3

Continue rolling and stretching the dough until it is about 1mm thick, which is not easy unless you have a long rolling pin. *[The rolling and stretching motion is illustrated in Figures 4 and 5.]* This rolled-out circle of pasta dough is called the *sfoglia*.

If you are making lasagne or stuffed pasta (such as ravioli or cannelloni), you must proceed to make it immediately. For lasagne or cannelloni, cut the dough into rectangles measuring about 20 x 10cm/ 8 x 4 inches. For ravioli or other stuffed shapes, see individual recipes.

Fig.4

If you are making any other kind of pasta (such as fettuccine, tagliatelle, pappardelle, garganelli), place a clean, dry towel on a table and lay the *sfoglia* on it to dry, letting about a third of the dough hang over the edge of the table. Turn every 10 minutes. The drying should take about 30 minutes, depending on the room temperature. The pasta dough is ready to cut when it is dry to the touch and begins to look leathery. Make sure that it does not get too dry, or it will become brittle and break when you fold and cut it. To cut the dough into strands, fold it over on itself three or four times and use a long, sharp knife to cut strips of the required width *[see Fig. 6]*.

Fig.5

Fig.6

Using a hand-cranked machine

Divide the dough into balls the size of oranges. Work on one ball at a time, leaving the others to rest, wrapped in clingfilm. Adjust the smooth kneading rollers of the machine to their widest setting, and pass the ball through six or seven times, folding it over and turning it 90 degrees after each rolling. Whenever the dough sticks to the rollers, sprinkle the rollers with flour. After six or seven times, do not fold the sheet any more. Adjust the rollers to the next thinnest setting, and pass the dough through once. Repeat for each remaining roller setting, passing the unfolded sheet once through each of them. If the strip of dough gets too long (more than 50cm/20 inches or so), cut it in half and proceed with one half at a time.

For tagliolini, tagliatelle or pappardelle, stop at the last but one setting. For flat sheet pasta or stuffed pasta, go through the last setting. However, if the atmosphere is damp or your kitchen too cold, you might find it difficult to stuff the pasta, in which case the last but one setting is safer. Only experience can guide you. Leave each sheet of dough between two clean tea towels while you repeat the process with the remaining balls of dough.

If you are making lasagne, cannelloni or stuffed pasta, proceed immediately. For lasagne or cannelloni, cut the dough into rectangles about 20 x 10cm/ 8 x 4 inches. For stuffed pasta, see individual recipe.

For tagliolini, tagliatelle or pappardelle, allow the rolled-out sheets of dough to dry as for hand-rolled pasta (see opposite) and then:

• for tagliolini, pass each sheet through the narrowest cutting blades, separate the strands, and leave until you are ready to cook – ideally on the same day, but not more than 2 days.

• for tagliatelle and pappardelle, pass the sheets through the broad cutting blades, separate, and leave until you are ready to cook.

Coloured pasta

The only traditional coloured pasta is the green one. All the others are modern fancy variations, which I don't think are worth considering.

To make the green colour, a small quantity of spinach is added to the dough. The primary purpose of the spinach is to colour the dough and, although the taste is not affected very much, it helps to make the pasta creamier and softer. The cooking time for spinach pasta is slightly longer. This green *sfoglia* is usually used for tagliatelle or lasagne.

150g/5½oz/generous ¾ cup cooked spinach
  or frozen spinach, thawed and cooked
  for 3 minutes

225g/8oz/1¾ cups Italian 00 flour

2 eggs

a pinch of fine sea salt

Squeeze all the liquid out of the spinach with your hands, and then chop it very finely with a knife or a mezzaluna.

Proceed as for homemade pasta (page 59), adding the spinach with the eggs to the well of the flour.

Cooking homemade pasta

Homemade pasta cooks in very little time, so have everything ready for serving before you drop the pasta into the boiling water.

You need a large, deep, cylindrical saucepan, and the same amount of water and salt as for dried pasta. For 400g/14oz of pasta you need to bring 4 litres/7 pints/ 4 quarts of water to the boil with 2 tablespoons of salt.

When the water is boiling very rapidly, drop in all the pasta at once. (For lasagne or cannelloni, see page 164 or page 191; for ravioli and other stuffed pasta, the water should boil steadily, but not too fast, or the pasta might break). Stir with a wooden spoon and quickly bring the water back to the boil. The cooking time varies according to the thickness of the pasta; usually about 2–3 minutes, but start testing after about 1 minute. Always reserve some of the pasta cooking water to add to the sauce, if necessary.

Key ingredients

Herbs

The herbs most frequently used in pasta sauces are basil, oregano, parsley and sage. All herbs are used fresh, except for oregano, which is generally used dried.

Olive oil

The oil used in pasta sauce is always olive oil. Extra virgin olive oil is needed when the oil is used raw or with very few other ingredients, such as in the recipe for spaghetti with oil, garlic and chilli (page 137), or spaghetti alla puttanesca (page 154). Regular olive oil can be used when the oil is mixed with other fats, as in the recipe for pappardelle with hare (page 95).

Garlic

Garlic is an important character in the pasta scenario, although not by any means an essential one. It is used a lot, but not in every sauce, and when used it is used with discretion.

It is always peeled before use; it may then be added either lightly crushed but whole and then removed, or chopped and left in the sauce. The thinner the garlic is cut, the stronger it tastes. When sautéing, garlic should not be allowed to become brown, or it will taste bitter.

When I use garlic that is no longer fresh, I cut the clove in half and remove the green germ, or shoot, which is the more pungent part of the garlic.

Parmesan cheese

Grated Parmesan is essential in many pasta sauces and is used in quite a few others, even if not essential. However, it is not needed in fish sauces – with the exception of some prawn sauces – nor in plain tomato sauces, such as the Neapolitan tomato sauce (page 72), and any sauces using raw tomatoes.

Always use fresh Italian Parmigiano-Reggiano, or Grana Padano, which is another good grating cheese.

Buy Parmesan in whole pieces and grate just before use. Store pieces of Parmesan in the refrigerator, well wrapped in foil. If the cheese becomes very hard and dry, wrap it in a damp cloth for a day and then put it back in the foil in the refrigerator.

Mozzarella cheese

There are two kinds of mozzarella: buffalo mozzarella (*mozzarella di bufala*) and cow mozzarella (which correctly is called *fior di latte*). Buffalo mozzarella has the slightly acidic flavour typical of this cheese, while cows' milk mozzarella is blander. You can use cows' milk mozzarella in some recipes, but when mozzarella is one of the main ingredients, as in the pasticcio di pasta alla napoletana (page 171), buffalo mozzarella should be used. I usually specify which one to use.

Ricotta salata

Ricotta salata is ricotta made from sheep's milk, slightly salted and hung until dry. It is widely used in Sicily and in southern Italy, usually grated, just like Parmesan and pecorino. It is difficult to find outside Italy, but can be bought in some Italian delis and online.

Tomatoes

Tomatoes to be used in sauces should be ripe, yet firm. Plum tomatoes are best because they have fewer seeds and more flesh than other varieties. However, it is often better to use canned tomatoes in sauces than fresh ones. The best-quality canned tomatoes are San Marzano, a variety especially grown for canning.

Concentrated tomato paste is no substitute for either fresh or canned tomatoes, but it can add an extra dimension to some sauces, increase the tomato flavour and help to bind.

Before they are used in a sauce, fresh tomatoes should always be peeled and the seeds discarded. To peel them, make a small incision in each tomato, drop into a small pan of rapidly boiling water and turn the heat off. Leave for 20–30 seconds (no longer, or they will start to cook) and then lift them out using a slotted spoon and put them into a bowl of cold water. The skin should come off very easily. Cut each tomato in half, discard the seeds and then roughly chop, dice or cut into strips, according to the recipe.

Pancetta

Chopped pancetta – fried together with onion and celery, and sometimes carrot and garlic – is the starting point for many pasta sauces. It is exactly the same cut of meat as streaky bacon, namely the belly of a pig, but is cured differently and is usually cut in thicker pieces rather than thin slices. As with streaky bacon, it can be smoked or green (unsmoked). Pasta sauces usually use the unsmoked pancetta. It is widely sold in supermarkets, but if you can't find it, use unsmoked streaky bacon instead.

Olio santo ('holy oil')

This flavoured oil – I don't know why it's called 'holy oil'– is made in southern Italy, where it is often put on the table for everybody to sprinkle on their salad, their fish, their pasta or whatever. This is how I make it, but you can add more or fewer chillies, depending on how hot you want it to be: to 500ml/18fl oz/2 cups of good olive oil, I add 3–4 seeded chillies, and leave it 4–5 days before beginning to use it.

Pasta recipes from the past

I think the following recipes are more interesting as historical documentation of pasta cooking outside Italy than as recipes you'd actually want to make. Pasta was usually thought of as a pudding, or accompanied by a white sauce, more like sloppy nursery food than the pasta eaten in Italy.

In the late nineteenth century pasta began to grow in popularity outside Italy, where it was by then rapidly becoming a staple food of the masses. The variety of ways in which it was served depended as much on economic circumstances as on climatic differences. The upper classes of England and America were serving most of their macaroni dishes as 'nursery food' for their children. They were usually bland, sweet puddings which the children loved because they were sweet and easy to chew.

Macaroni with Parmesan cheese

One of the first pasta recipes to appear in England came from *The Cook's Paradise* by William Verral, published in 1759. Verral was an innkeeper, who learned his art as a boy under the great chef St Clouet. In his book Verral includes two sweet pasta recipes and the following savoury one. I am indebted to the late Elizabeth David for drawing my attention to this book.

'These are to be had at any confectioner's in London and the newer they are the better – this is not what we call macaroons of the sweet biscuit sort, but a foreign paste, the same as vermicelly, but made very large in comparison to that – for this you must boil them in water first, with a little salt, pour on them a ladle of coulis, a morsel of green onion and parsley minced fine, pepper, salt and nutmeg: stew all a few minutes, and pour into a dish with a rim, squeeze a lemon or orange, and cover it pretty thick with Parmesan cheese grated very fine, bake it of a fine colour, about a quarter of an hour, and serve it up hot.'

If you'd like to re-create this dish, my suggested ingredients for 4 persons are:

350g/12oz macaroni
125ml/4fl oz/½ cup gravy thickened with
    1 teaspoon Italian 00 flour
55g/2oz/4 tbsp unsalted butter
1 tbsp finely chopped onion
2 tbsp chopped flat-leaf parsley
¼ tsp grated nutmeg
salt and pepper
the grated rind and juice of ½ lemon or orange
75g/2¾oz Parmesan cheese, grated

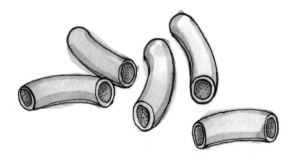

Baked vermicelli

This recipe, from a nineteenth-century English cookbook, is quite good, although I have not been able to find out the difference between the Genoese vermicelli and the Neapolitan ones. I presume it was their thickness.

'Simmer 4 ounces of vermicelli in a pint of new milk 10 minutes. Then put to it ½ pint of cream, a teaspoonful of pounded cinnamon, 4 ounces of butter warmed, the same of white sugar, and the yolks of 4 eggs well beaten: a little oil of almonds or a couple of spoonfuls of ratafia will much improve the flavour. Bake in a dish without lining: but observe that of the two sorts of vermicelli the Genoese will require ¾ and the Neapolitan only ½ an hour of baking.'

Boiled vermicelli

A variation on a pasta pudding, from the same book as the previous recipe.

'Stir very gently 4 ounces of vermicelli into a pint of new milk over the stove, until it be scalding hot, but not more: then pour it into a basin and add to it, while hot, 1 ounce of butter and 2 of sugar. When the above is nearly cold, mix in, very gently, 2 well-beaten eggs: and immediately put it into a basin which will exactly hold it. Cover carefully with a floured cloth: and turning the basin the narrow end upwards, move it around for 10 minutes and boil for an hour. Serve with pudding sauce.'

Baked macaroni

From a nineteenth-century American cookbook:

'Simmer 1 or 2 ounces of the pipe sort in 2 cups of milk, and a bit of lemon and cinnamon, till tender: put it into a dish with the milk, 2 or 3 yolks of eggs, but only 1 white, sugar, nutmeg, 1 spoonful of peach-water or almond milk and a glass of raisin wine. Bake with a paste round the edges.

A layer of orange marmalade or raspberry jam at the bottom of a macaroni pudding, for change, is a great improvement, in which case omit the almond or peach-water, which you would otherwise flavor it with, or a glass of brandy.'

Vegetable pie

A savoury nursery dish of 1860, which I think sounds pretty good:

'Boil some vermicelli and strain it. Have some onions chopped fine, and fry until slightly brown in a little butter. Have some eggs hard boiled and some tomatoes cut in slices. Put a layer of tomatoes in the bottom of a pie dish, then some onions and a layer of eggs, cut in slices. Then the vermicelli. Cover with some 'nice white sauce' and a little chopped parsley, picked fresh from the herb garden, and on the top of all some slices of potatoes. Put in the oven and bake for about half an hour until the potatoes are brown on the top.'

Basic sauces

All these sauces can be used by themselves or
as a base for more elaborate dishes. They can all be
made in advance and stored in the refrigerator for
up to 4 or 5 days, or frozen. The two meat sauces
(*ragù*) are perfect for short or homemade pasta,
while the tomato sauces are better for spaghetti,
linguine or any long pasta. All the sauces are for
dressing 350g/12oz of pasta,
4 first-course helpings.

Ragù alla bolognese

{ Bolognese meat sauce }

For 4 helpings of pasta

30g/1oz/2 tbsp unsalted
  butter

4 tbsp olive oil

50g/1¾oz pancetta, cubed

1 onion, finely chopped

1 carrot, finely chopped

1 celery stalk, finely chopped

50g/1¾oz chicken livers,
  cleaned and cut into
  small pieces

2 tsp tomato purée (paste)

350g/12oz lean minced
  (ground) beef

250ml/9fl oz/1 cup red wine

1 bay leaf

500ml/18fl oz/2 cups
  meat stock

salt and freshly ground
  black pepper

a grating of nutmeg

This is the classic sauce used in Bologna for baked lasagne and for tagliatelle. You can use stock made with good-quality meat bouillon. There are as many versions of ragù as there are cooks. This recipe here contains chicken livers, one of the traditional ingredients in some provinces of Emilia, but if you don't like them, leave them out. The important thing is that ragù should cook for a long time.

Heat the butter and oil together in a heavy saucepan. When hot, throw in the pancetta and cook over high heat until brown. Add the onion and fry for about 5 minutes. Add the carrot and celery and cook for 5 minutes, then add the chicken livers and cook for 2–3 minutes, turning them over frequently. Stir in the tomato purée and cook for 1 minute, stirring the whole time.

Add the beef, increase the heat and cook rapidly until the meat is just beginning to lose its raw look, stirring thoroughly to break up the clumps of meat. Add the wine and the bay leaf and cook over high heat until the wine has boiled briskly for 2–3 minutes, stirring constantly.

Pour in half the stock, mix well and add salt, pepper and nutmeg. Simmer over very low heat for at least 2 hours. Keep an eye on it and whenever the ragù gets too dry add a little of the remaining stock. Remove the bay leaf before using the sauce.

Variations
- *You can use half minced beef and half minced pork.*
- *If the ragù becomes too dry during the long cooking, you can add some whole milk instead of stock.*

Ragù alla napoletana

{ Neapolitan meat sauce }

Serves 6

4 tbsp olive oil

1kg/2lb 4oz braising steak
in a single piece, such
as brisket

1 onion, finely chopped

3 garlic cloves, finely
chopped

250ml/9fl oz/1 cup red wine

400g/14oz canned chopped
tomatoes

2 tbsp tomato purée (paste),
diluted in 4 tbsp hot water

½ tsp ground cloves

1 tsp ground cinnamon

½ tsp grated nutmeg

salt and freshly ground
black pepper

This ragù is made with a piece of braising beef cooked at length. It is the traditional meat sauce used in Naples to dress pasta, where the meat is often served sliced as a second course, the pasta being dressed with most of the cooking juices and served as the first course.

Heat 1 tablespoon of the oil in a casserole and brown the meat on all sides. Do this carefully and well, since it is quite an important step. When this is done, remove the meat from the pan and set aside.

Add the remaining oil and the onion to the pan and sauté for 5 minutes, stirring frequently. Add the garlic and sauté for a further minute. Return the meat to the pan and pour in the wine. Boil briskly for 2–3 minutes and then add the tomatoes and the diluted tomato purée. Bring to the boil, then turn down the heat and add the spices, salt and pepper. Place the lid askew over the pan to allow some steam to escape, and cook very gently for 2½–3 hours, until the meat is very tender. Turn the meat over every 30 minutes or so and, if necessary, add a little hot water: the meat should cook in enough liquid to come about halfway up its side.

When the meat is very tender, turn off the heat. The lovely red liquid in the pot is the Neapolitan ragù.

Sugo di pomodoro

{ Plain tomato sauce }

For 4–6 helpings of pasta

1kg/2lb 4oz fresh tomatoes,
  peeled, seeded and
  quartered, or 2 x 400g/14oz
  cans plum tomatoes

1 onion, quartered

1 small celery stalk,
  cut into pieces

1 garlic clove

1 bay leaf

a large sprig of parsley

1 tsp tomato purée (paste)

1 tsp sugar

salt and freshly ground
  black pepper

This tomato sauce can be used on its own, or as a base for sauces that include other ingredients. Add a kilo of clams (*vongole verace*/palourdes) and you have a perfect sauce for a dish of spaghetti alle vongole, or throw in three or four cleaned and sliced squid, or some small fried meatballs.

Put all the ingredients in a saucepan and boil over moderate heat, uncovered, until the onion is soft, approximately 30 minutes, stirring every now and then to prevent sticking.

    Remove the bay leaf and whizz the sauce in a food processor. If you wish to use the sauce at once, simply reheat gently and pour it over freshly cooked pasta that has been tossed with olive oil and/or butter.

Sugo di pomodoro alla napoletana

{ Neapolitan tomato sauce }

For 3–4 helpings of pasta

1kg/2lb 4oz fresh tomatoes,
  peeled, seeded and chopped

2 garlic cloves, chopped

5 tbsp olive oil

salt and freshly ground black
  pepper

a dozen fresh basil leaves,
  torn into small pieces

This sauce should be made with fresh tomatoes, which must be ripe and full of flavour. Plum tomatoes are the best because they contain few seeds and have a lot of juicy flesh.

Combine the tomatoes, garlic, olive oil, salt and pepper in a saucepan and boil over moderately high heat, uncovered, for about 7–10 minutes or until the oil has separated from the tomatoes. Throw in the basil and check the seasoning.

Sugo di pomodoro all'emiliana

{ Emilian tomato sauce }

For 3–4 helpings of pasta

30g/1oz/2 tbsp unsalted
  butter

4 tbsp olive oil

1 small onion, chopped

1 celery stalk, chopped

1 garlic clove

500g/1lb 2oz fresh tomatoes,
  peeled and seeded, or
  400g/14oz canned chopped
  tomatoes

1 tbsp tomato purée (paste)

1 tsp sugar

125ml/4fl oz/½ cup red wine

salt and freshly ground
  black pepper

2 tbsp chopped flat-leaf
  parsley

While the Neapolitan tomato sauce (page 72) is particularly good for spaghetti, this Emilian sauce is better with homemade pasta or short pasta, such as macaroni or penne.

Heat the butter and oil together in a saucepan. When hot, throw in the onion, celery and garlic and sauté them until soft, about 7–8 minutes.

Add the tomatoes (if you use canned tomatoes, discard some of the juice), the tomato purée, sugar, wine, salt and pepper and cook, uncovered, for about 45 minutes, stirring every now and then.

Blitz the sauce in a food processor and then add the parsley. Taste and check the seasoning.

Béchamel sauce

**Makes about 500ml/
18fl oz/2 cups**

750ml/1¼ pints/3 cups
  whole milk
60g/2¼oz/4 tbsp unsalted
  butter
50–60g/1¾–2¼oz/6 tbsp
  Italian 00 flour
salt and freshly ground
  black pepper

Béchamel is a simple sauce and can be made very quickly. Like some other sauces that were supposedly created in the seventeenth century by the French, béchamel was allegedly already known in Italy, under the name *balsamella*. It was a sauce made from milk, flour and butter, and it was a vital ingredient of many pasta dishes, especially those made with lasagne.

This makes a medium-thick sauce. For a thicker sauce, increase the quantities of butter and flour, but make sure that you always use slightly more butter.

In a small saucepan, slowly bring the milk to simmering point.

Meanwhile, melt the butter over very low heat in a heavy-bottomed saucepan. When the butter has melted, add the flour and stir well with a wooden spoon; cook, stirring constantly, until the mixture is just golden, but not brown.

Remove from the heat and add the hot milk, a few tablespoons at a time, until all the milk has been incorporated and the sauce is smooth. Add salt and pepper. Return the saucepan to the heat and slowly bring the sauce to the boil, stirring the whole time. Simmer for about 5 minutes for a medium-thick sauce, or 6–7 minutes for a thicker sauce. If the sauce has some lumps, blitz in a food processor for a few seconds to break up any lumps.

If you do not wish to use the sauce immediately, lay a sheet of clingfilm over the top to prevent a skin from forming. Béchamel can be kept in the refrigerator for 2 or 3 days. When you want to use it, add a lump of butter and 2–3 tablespoons of milk and reheat gently, stirring well with a wooden spoon.

Flavourings
- *Nutmeg is the most common flavouring; a little grating can be added with the salt and pepper.*
- *For a garlic-flavoured sauce, add 1 crushed garlic clove to the milk when it is being heated, and remove before adding the milk to the butter and flour mixture. No nutmeg is used in this case.*
- *For an onion-flavoured sauce, sauté, very gently, 1 tablespoon of grated onion in the butter. When cooked (about 3 minutes), add the flour and proceed as above.*

Sugo crudo per spaghetti

{ Uncooked tomato sauce for spaghetti }

For 3–4 helpings of spaghetti

500g/1lb 2oz fresh ripe
tomatoes, peeled
and seeded

5 tbsp extra virgin olive oil

1 garlic clove, finely chopped

10–12 fresh basil leaves, each
torn into 2 or 3 pieces,
or 2 tbsp finely chopped
fresh parsley

salt and freshly ground
black pepper

This sauce is very easy to make, but needs really good tomatoes, fresh herbs and good-quality extra virgin olive oil. It is fun to create new tastes by substituting herbs or adding different ingredients to the basic mixture.

Chop the tomatoes and place in a shallow ovenproof bowl with the other ingredients. Stir well. Leave to marinate for at least 2 hours. It does not matter if you leave the sauce to marinate for longer.

   Preheat the oven to 150°C/300°F/gas mark 2. Cook your spaghetti and, while the pasta is cooking, put the bowl with the sauce in the oven. When the spaghetti is ready, drain – do not overdrain – and turn it into the bowl, mix well and serve immediately. No cheese is necessary with this sauce.

Variations
Combine all the ingredients except the olive oil in the blender. Blend to a smooth sauce. When the pasta is cooked, toss it first with the oil and then with the sauce. Add ½ tsp crushed dried chillies, 2 tbsp capers and 50g/1¾oz/4 tbsp pitted black olives, roughly chopped, to the tomatoes.

Soups

The following recipes are for substantial soups, to which a handful or two of pasta are added for both nourishment and a different texture. A soup that is simplicity itself and needs no recipe is *minestrina*, which consists of clear stock – chicken, light meat or vegetable – to which some small pasta shapes, or *pastina*, such as stelline, alfabeto or risone, are added. It is a classic of northern Italian cooking.

La minestra di Orazio

{ Horace's chickpea, laganelle and leek soup }

Serves 6

200g/7oz/1 cup dried
   chickpeas

1 leek (white part only),
   cut into rings and
   thoroughly washed

1 celery stalk, chopped

1 bay leaf, crushed

salt and freshly ground
   black pepper

200g/7oz laganelle or
   mafalde

6 tbsp extra virgin olive oil

bunch of flat-leaf parsley,
   chopped

In ancient Rome, pasta made with durum wheat flour and water was baked on large, hot, porous stones. It was then cut into strips and used in soup. Sometimes it was fried instead of baked. This recipe is my interpretation of the dish to which the poet Horace refers in one of his *Satires*, 'Ad porri et ciceris refero, laganique catinum' ('I am going home to a bowl of leeks and chickpeas and lasagne'). It is one of the earliest references to any kind of pasta. Here I have used laganelle, long strips of pasta about 3cm/ 1¼ inches wide. Mafalde, sometimes called lasagnette or reginette, are slightly narrower and have fluted edges.

You should not use canned chickpeas for this soup because the flavour of any soup comes mainly from the stock. Cooking the dried chickpeas produces a stock with the mealy, earthy flavour of the chickpeas, which would never be found in a soup made with canned chickpeas.

Soak the chickpeas overnight in plenty of cold water. Drain them and rinse them with fresh water.

Put the chickpeas into a large saucepan. Add 1.5 litres/2½ pints/1½ quarts of cold water, the leek, celery, bay leaf and a good quantity of freshly ground pepper – but no salt, or the chickpea skins will harden. Cover the pan tightly, and bring the liquid rapidly to the boil. Reduce the heat and simmer until the chickpeas are tender, which may take up to 2½ hours. Do not uncover the pan, or the chickpeas will become hard and will not cook through.

Cook the pasta and drain when slightly undercooked. While the pasta is cooking, heat the oil in a large frying pan. Turn the drained pasta into the oil and stir-fry for about 2 minutes. Scoop all the pasta and oil into the chickpea soup, season with salt and pepper to taste and cook until the pasta is tender. Ladle into individual bowls and sprinkle with the parsley.

Minestrone di pasta

{ Minestrone with pasta }

Serves 6–8

2 potatoes, diced

2 carrots, diced

2 celery stalks with the green
leaves attached, stringed
and diced

2 small courgettes (zucchini),
diced

100g/3½oz green beans,
topped and tailed and cut
into 2–3cm/1 inch pieces

the outside leaves of a cos/
romaine lettuce, shredded

250g/9oz ripe tomatoes,
peeled and chopped

2 garlic cloves, chopped

225g/8oz/1 cup cooked
cannellini beans, or drained
beans from a can or carton

2 tsp vegetable bouillon
powder

salt and freshly ground
black pepper

150g/5½oz small tubular
pasta, such as ditalini or
pennette

about 6–8 tbsp extra virgin
olive oil, or half extra virgin
olive oil and half olio santo
(page 64)

half a dozen basil leaves, torn
into pieces

Don't let the long list of ingredients put you off: once you have cleaned and cut the vegetables, the rest is easy and you can go and sit down.

It is best to make minestrone in large quantity. It tastes even better reheated a day or two later and it keeps well in the fridge for 2 or 3 days, although it does not freeze well. Add the pasta only just before you are going to serve it. This minestrone is also delicious cold – not chilled, but at room temperature.

I like to add olio santo (page 64) to pasta minestrone. But if you do not have it, add some extra virgin olive oil and hand around a jar of crushed dried chillies.

Put all the vegetables in your stockpot, add 2 litres/3½ pints/2 quarts of water and bring slowly to the boil. Sprinkle in the bouillon powder and stir well. Simmer, uncovered, over very low heat for 1½–2 hours.

Add salt and pepper to taste and then throw in the pasta – if the soup seems too thick, add some boiling water before adding the pasta. Boil until the pasta is cooked and then ladle the soup into individual bowls. Pour a tablespoon or so of oil over each serving and scatter with the basil leaves.

Pasta e fagioli alla veneta

{ Pasta and borlotti beans soup }

Serves 4–5

200g/7oz/1 cup dried
  borlotti beans

4 tbsp olive oil

100g/3½oz unsmoked
  pancetta, chopped

1 small onion, chopped

1 celery stalk, chopped

1 garlic clove, chopped

2 litres/3½ pints/2 quarts
  beef or vegetable stock

400g/14oz canned chopped
  plum tomatoes

salt and freshly ground
  black pepper

200g/7oz ditalini or
  maltagliati

3 tbsp chopped flat-leaf
  parsley

freshly grated Parmesan
  cheese, to serve

This is a very thick peasant soup. Practically every region in Italy has its own variation. The recipe below, made with borlotti beans, is from the region around Venice, where the best borlotti beans grow; the variation from Naples is made with cannellini, the local beans. Maltagliati means 'badly cut' and refers to rolled-out pasta dough, which in the Veneto region is cut into small diamond shapes.

This soup is made with dried beans, or fresh beans when they are in season. It is never made with canned beans because you need the flavour of the stock in which the beans have cooked.

Soak the beans overnight in cold water. Drain and rinse them with fresh water.

Heat the oil in a large saucepan, add the pancetta and sauté until crisp. Add the onion, celery and garlic and sauté for 2 minutes. Add the beans and cook for 1 minute, stirring constantly, and then cover with 1.5 litres/2½ pints/1½ quarts of the stock. Cover the pan and simmer for 1 hour over very low heat.

Add the tomatoes, salt and pepper to the pan, but be careful not to add too much salt, as the beans absorb a great quantity of the liquid. Simmer, covered, until the beans are really tender; this may take another hour or more, depending on how long the beans have been stored.

Using a slotted spoon, scoop out about half the beans and put them into a food processor. Blitz to a purée and then return the purée to the pan and mix well. Bring the soup back to the boil and add more boiling stock or water before you throw in the ditalini. Put the lid back on the pan and boil until the pasta is cooked.

Add the parsley and leave the soup to rest for about 2 minutes before serving. Hand around a bowl of grated Parmesan.

Variation: The Neapolitan recipe
The pasta used for this soup is munnezzaglia, *a name given to pasta of different shapes all mixed together – an ingenious way to use up the remaining small quantities of different packets. Long pasta, such as ziti or bucatini, is cut into short pieces and mixed with short pasta.*

The ingredients are very similar to those in the previous recipe, but you must leave out the pancetta and the onion and celery, and use cannellini beans instead of borlotti. Increase the garlic to 3 cloves and use water instead of stock – you might like to add 2 teaspoons of vegetable bouillon powder for more flavour. You will need 5 tablespoons of olive oil and, at the end, 2 tablespoons of olio santo (page 64) together with half a dozen torn basil leaves instead of the parsley.

Put the water in the saucepan. Add the beans (previously soaked overnight), garlic, tomatoes, salt and a good quantity of pepper. Simmer, covered, until the beans are tender, about 1½ hours.

Add the oil and the pasta and boil gently, covered, until the pasta is cooked. If the beans have absorbed most of the water, you may have to add more boiling water before adding the pasta. Ladle the soup into individual bowls, drizzle with some olio santo and scatter a few pieces of basil in each bowl. This soup is also excellent cold. No cheese is served with this version.

Pasta e lenticchie

{ Lentil and pasta soup }

Serves 6

6 tbsp olive oil

2 garlic cloves, chopped

125g/4½oz unsmoked pancetta, cubed

250g/9oz/1¼ cups Castelluccio or Puy lentils, rinsed and drained

1.5 litres/2½ pints/1½ quarts meat stock

200g/7oz tortiglioni or rigatoni

3 tbsp chopped fresh parsley

salt and freshly ground black pepper

Lentils are eaten in most parts of Italy and are a traditional dish served on New Year's Day, because they supposedly bring riches and wealth throughout the New Year, one lentil representing one golden coin.

Heat half the oil in a large saucepan, add the garlic and the pancetta and sauté for 5 minutes, stirring all the time. Throw in the lentils and cook over gentle heat for 2–3 minutes.

Pour in the stock, bring to the boil and cook, covered, for about 15–20 minutes. The exact time depends on the variety of lentil and how long they have been stored – the older they are, the longer they will take to cook. At this stage the lentils should be slightly undercooked.

Now add the pasta, put the lid back on the pan and cook until the pasta is done. Pour in the remaining oil and mix well. Season with salt and pepper to taste. Ladle the soup into individual bowls and sprinkle with the parsley.

This soup is usually served without cheese, but a bowl of grated Parmesan might be welcome.

Minestra di fave

{ Broad beans and pasta soup }

Serves 6

3 tbsp extra virgin olive oil

1 large red onion,
  cut into rings

2 garlic cloves, chopped

2 tbsp tomato purée (paste)

1 bay leaf

500g/1lb 2oz shelled fresh
  young broad (fava) beans,
  or frozen or canned
  broad beans

1.5 litres/2½ pints/1½ quarts
  chicken or vegetable stock

salt and freshly ground
  black pepper

125g/4½oz ditalini or other
  small pasta shapes

2 tbsp olio santo (page 64)

2 tbsp ricotta

freshly grated Parmesan
  cheese, to serve (optional)

This is a traditional soup from Tuscany, a region that boasts the best broad beans and the best recipes for them.

Heat the oil in a large saucepan, add the onion and garlic and sauté for 5 minutes. Add the tomato purée and the bay leaf and cook for 1 minute. Throw in the broad beans and cook for 2 minutes, stirring constantly. Cover with the stock, add salt and pepper, and cook until the beans are tender, about 5 minutes.

When the broad beans are cooked, remove the bay leaf and lift out about half of the beans, using a slotted spoon; remove the outer skins of the beans. Also lift out as many onion rings as possible and add to the peeled broad beans.

If you want a very smooth soup, you will have to purée the rest of the soup through a food mill. Or you can blitz it in a food processor, but you will then feel the tiny bits of skin in the soup.

Return the puréed soup to the saucepan, add the pasta and boil gently until it is cooked. Add the peeled broad beans and the onion rings and ladle into individual soup bowls. Dribble with the olio santo and spoon a little of the ricotta in the middle of each bowl.

A bowl of grated Parmesan can be served on the side, if you like.

Pasta e ceci

{ Pasta and chickpea soup }

Serves 6

175g/6oz/generous ¾ cup dried chickpeas

1.5–2 litres/2½–3½ pints/ 1½–2 quarts vegetable stock or water

1 bay leaf

2 garlic cloves, chopped

125ml/4fl oz/½ cup extra virgin olive oil

salt and freshly ground black pepper

175g/6oz elbow macaroni or other small short pasta

freshly grated Parmesan cheese, to serve (optional)

This is a more modern version – although it is still very old – of the soup mentioned by Horace, as described on page 78. In even later versions, tomatoes are added. The soup must be made with dried chickpeas – not with canned ones – because you use the liquid in which they have cooked, which has that lovely and distinctive mealy flavour of the chickpeas.

This soup can be made ahead of time up to the stage of adding the pasta; it can then be refrigerated or frozen.

Soak the chickpeas in water overnight – changing the water once, if you remember.

Drain the chickpeas and rinse them in fresh water. Put them into a good-sized, heavy-bottomed saucepan (ideally earthenware), add the stock or water, bay leaf, garlic, oil and pepper – but no salt, or the chickpea skins will harden. Cover tightly and bring the soup rapidly to the boil. Reduce the heat and simmer until the chickpeas are tender; this usually takes at least 2 hours, but the time will vary, depending on how long the chickpeas have been stored. Do not uncover the pan for the first hour or so, or the chickpeas will become hard and will not cook properly.

When the chickpeas are tender, add salt and the pasta and boil gently until it is cooked. You might also have to add some boiling water; it depends on how much liquid has evaporated. Taste and adjust the seasoning. When the pasta is cooked, leave the soup to rest for 5 minutes before serving. A bowl of grated Parmesan can be served on the side.

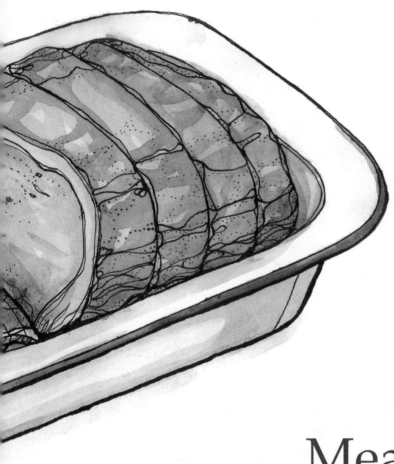

Meat
and poultry

The following recipes are for pasta dishes
containing meat. Sometimes the meat plays a
supporting role – to eggs, peas, asparagus – and
sometimes it is a dominant ingredient. Quite a few
of these dishes would work very well as a one-dish
meal, which can be followed by a salad of some
sort. But this is for you to decide.

Bucatini alla carbonara

{ Bucatini with eggs and bacon }

Serves 4

1 tbsp olive oil

115g/4oz unsmoked
  pancetta, cubed

350g/12oz bucatini

4 egg yolks

100g/3½oz pecorino cheese,
  grated

30g/1oz/2 tbsp unsalted
  butter, melted

salt and freshly ground
  black pepper

The origins of this now-famous sauce are not at all clear. The most likely is that it was made by the *carbonari* – charcoal burners – when they were working up in the mountains east of Rome. Whatever its origin, bucatini alla carbonara became a very popular dish all over Italy after the Second World War and was soon known all over the western world. It should be made with *guanciale* (pig's jowl cured in the same way as pancetta), which is a traditional pork product from Lazio, but pancetta is a good substitute.

Preheat the oven to 120°C/250°F/gas mark ½.

Heat the oil in a frying pan and when hot, throw in the pancetta. Cook for about 10 minutes or until the pancetta is brown and crisp. While the pancetta is cooking, cook the pasta in boiling salted water.

In a bowl, beat together the egg yolks, cheese, butter, salt and lots of black pepper. Place the bowl in the oven.

When the pasta is ready, drain, reserving a cupful of the water, and turn it into the frying pan with the pancetta. Using two forks, stir-fry until all the strands are well coated with the fat, adding a few tablespoons of the pasta water to loosen them. Transfer to the warmed bowl with the egg mixture, mix thoroughly and serve at once on warmed plates.

Variations
• *Add 4 or 5 fresh sage leaves, torn, to the pancetta while it is being sautéed.*
• *You can use 3 whole eggs, instead of 4 yolks.*
• *Add 2–3 tablespoons of dry white wine to the pancetta and quickly evaporate for a richer flavour.*

Taglierini con piselli, prosciutto cotto e panna

{ Taglierini with peas, ham and cream }

Serves 4

60g/2¼oz/4 tbsp unsalted
  butter

200g/7oz/1½ cups shelled
  peas or frozen petits pois

200ml/7fl oz/generous ¾ cup
  vegetable stock

150g/5½oz cooked ham,
  thickly sliced and cut
  into matchsticks

4 tbsp double (heavy) cream

salt

a generous grating of nutmeg

350g/12oz taglierini

100g/3½oz Parmesan cheese,
  grated

This creamy sauce is perfect for a dish of fine taglierini, although you could use tagliatelle or reginette. If you do not have any stock to hand, make it with vegetable bouillon powder. This sauce does not really need pepper, but add it if you like.

Heat the butter in a small saucepan and when the butter has melted, add the peas and half the stock. Put the lid on the pan and cook very gently until the peas are done, adding more stock as necessary, so that the peas are always cooking in some liquid. Mix in the ham and the cream and season with salt and nutmeg.

While the peas are cooking, cook the taglierini, which takes only 2 minutes to be ready.

Reserve a cupful of the pasta water and drain the pasta, without shaking the colander too much.

Fork out half of the taglierini and transfer to a warmed bowl. Spoon some sauce, a little of the pasta water and sprinkle some Parmesan over them and mix well, using two forks to separate the strands. Add the remaining taglierini, the rest of the sauce and a little more Parmesan and mix well again. If necessary, add a little more pasta water. Serve with more grated Parmesan handed around in a bowl.

Tagliolini con gli asparagi

{ Tagliolini with asparagus }

Serves 4

homemade tagliolini
 (pages 58–61) made with
 200g/7oz Italian 00 flour
 and 2 eggs, or 300g/10½oz
 dried egg tagliolini or
 tagliatelle

500g/1lb 2oz asparagus

salt and freshly ground black
 pepper (optional)

30g/1oz/2 tbsp unsalted
 butter

1 tbsp olive oil

2 tbsp grated onion

150ml/5fl oz/⅔ cup
 double (heavy) cream

a grating of nutmeg

150g/5½oz prosciutto,
 thickly sliced

50g/1¾oz Parmesan cheese,
 grated

For this sauce you need thickly cut prosciutto, not the pre-packed wafer-thin slices.

If you are making the pasta at home, follow the instructions on pages 58–61.

Trim off the hard stalks of the asparagus. For this dish you need only about 8cm/3 inches of the tip ends (you can keep the rest of the stalks to make a soup). Wash the tips and then boil them in salted water for 3 minutes. Drain and pour the asparagus water into a large pot for the pasta. Add more water and more salt to the asparagus water and bring back to the boil, ready to cook the pasta.

Heat the butter and oil in a large frying pan, add the onion and sauté for 5 minutes, stirring frequently so that the onion does not become golden, just soft. Cut the asparagus into 2cm/¾ inch lengths and add to the onion. Cook for a couple of minutes and then add the cream, nutmeg and some pepper if you like. If the pasta is not ready, take the pan off the heat or the asparagus tips will overcook.

While the sauce is cooking, cook the tagliolini in the boiling water and when it is ready, drain, reserving some of the water. Turn the pasta immediately into the frying pan with the sauce. Add the prosciutto and 2–3 tablespoons of the Parmesan and, using two forks to separate the strands, stir-fry for a good 2 minutes, adding a little of the reserved water to get the right fluidity. Serve at once, with the remaining Parmesan on the side.

Variation
Instead of prosciutto you can use ham; it goes very well.

Penne alla pizzaiola di manzo

{ Penne with a pizza sauce and beef }

Serves 4

500g/1lb 2oz beef steak

30g/1oz/2 tbsp unsalted
butter

4 tbsp olive oil

2 garlic cloves, finely
chopped

500g/1lb 2oz fresh tomatoes,
peeled, seeded and
chopped, or canned plum
tomatoes

1 tbsp dried oregano

2 tbsp capers, rinsed

salt and freshly ground black
pepper

350g/12oz penne

freshly grated Parmesan
cheese, to serve

The penne, in this recipe more an accompaniment to the meat than vice versa,
are dressed with a kind of pizza sauce containing strips of beef. You do not
need to use beef fillet; I use feather steak – the French *onglet* – whenever I can
find it.

Cut the meat into very thin slices, and then into strips, approximately 5 x 1cm/
2 inches x ½ inch.

Heat the butter and 2 tablespoons of the oil in a sauté pan. When the foam
subsides, add the garlic, sauté for 30 seconds and then add the strips of beef and
brown them quickly on all sides for no longer than 1 minute. Using a slotted
spoon, remove the meat from the pan and set aside.

Throw the tomatoes into the sauté pan and cook over moderately high heat
for about 10 minutes, or until the oil partly separates from the tomatoes. Add the
oregano, capers, salt and pepper to taste and then return the meat and all the
juices to the pan. Turn off the heat and cover the pan to keep the sauce warm.

While the sauce is cooking, cook the penne. When they are al dente, drain
them and return them to the pan in which they have cooked. Mix in the
remaining oil and some of the tomato sauce without the bits of meat.

Divide the penne among four warmed plates, top each mound of penne
with a quarter of the meat sauce and serve at once with a bowl of grated
Parmesan on the side.

Variations
* *Pound 3 or 4 anchovy fillets to a thick paste in a mortar, and add to the sauce
together with the tomatoes.*
* *Add 55g/2oz/4–5 tbsp pitted black olives to the tomato sauce.*

Tagliolini con animelle e prosciutto cotto

{ Tagliolini with sweetbreads and ham }

Serves 4

homemade tagliolini
(pages 58–61) made with
200g/7oz Italian 00 flour
and 2 eggs, or 300g/10½oz
dried egg tagliolini or
tagliatelle

250g/9oz calves' sweetbreads

100g/3½oz/scant ½ cup
unsalted butter

2 tbsp very finely chopped
shallot

salt and freshly ground
black pepper

6 tbsp dry Marsala

100g/3½oz cooked ham,
thickly sliced and cut into
short strips

1 tbsp fresh thyme leaves

a grating of nutmeg

125ml/4fl oz/½ cup double
(heavy) cream

freshly grated Parmesan
cheese, to serve

Sweetbreads are the most delicate of offal. The best are calves' sweetbreads, which you can buy online or from good butchers.

If you are making the pasta at home, follow the instructions on pages 58–61.

Put the sweetbreads in a bowl, cover with warm water and leave for 10 minutes. Drain them, put them in a saucepan and cover with fresh water. Bring the water to the boil and simmer for no longer than 2 minutes. Drain and leave them to get cold. Now peel off as much as you can of the thin membrane that covers them and remove all the bits of gristle without breaking them. Put them on a plate, cover with another plate, place some weight on it to press them down and leave for an hour or so. Slice them into pieces and then pat dry with kitchen paper.

Put a large pot of water on to boil for the pasta.

Heat half of the butter in a sauté pan and when the foam begins to subside, throw in the shallot and a pinch or two of salt. Sauté for 5 minutes, stirring frequently. Add the sweetbreads and continue cooking for 2 minutes. Pour in the Marsala, reduce over high heat, and then add the ham, thyme, nutmeg and salt and pepper. Cook, stirring, for 1 minute and then pour in the cream. Mix thoroughly, cover the pan and cook slowly for no more than 5 minutes. If the pasta is not ready, remove the pan from the heat and keep warm – overcooked sweetbreads become rubbery and hard.

While the sweetbreads are cooking, cook the tagliolini. When they are ready, drain, reserving a cupful of the water, and turn them into a warmed bowl. Add the remaining butter and, using two forks, toss to coat the strands in the butter, adding a little of the reserved water to loosen them. Spoon over some of the sauce and mix again, and then cover with the sweetbreads and the rest of the sauce. Serve at once, with plenty of grated Parmesan on the side.

Farfalle con i rognoncini

{ Farfalle with kidneys }

Serves 4

500g/1lb 2oz lambs' kidneys

3 tbsp wine vinegar

350g/12oz farfalle

2–3 tbsp Italian 00 flour

salt and freshly ground
  black pepper

4 tbsp olive oil

1 garlic clove,
  very finely chopped

4 tbsp dry sherry

125ml/4fl oz/½ cup double
  (heavy) cream

1½ tbsp lemon juice

50g/1¾oz/4 tbsp unsalted
  butter

3 tbsp chopped flat-leaf
  parsley

You can find lambs' kidneys in any butcher's shop. They are very good, full of flavour and make a delicious sauce for pasta.

Split the kidneys in half lengthwise and remove the core and as much of the membrane as you can. Cut the kidneys into strips, place them in a bowl, cover with cold water and add the vinegar. Soak for about 1 hour. Drain and pat dry with kitchen paper.

Drop the farfalle into rapidly boiling salted water and cook until al dente.

While the pasta is cooking, lightly coat the kidneys with the flour seasoned with a little salt. Heat the oil and the garlic in a frying pan. When the garlic begins to colour, add the kidneys and cook over moderate heat, stirring constantly for 1 minute. Pour in the sherry and boil rapidly for 1 minute. Turn the heat down and add the cream, lemon juice and salt and pepper to taste. Cook for about 2 minutes, stirring frequently and adding a little of the pasta cooking water. Do not overcook the kidneys, or they will become hard and rubbery. If they are ready before the pasta, remove the pan from the heat and keep warm.

When the pasta is ready, drain and return it to the pan in which it has cooked. Immediately add the butter and toss to coat, and then spoon the kidneys and their juices over the pasta. Sprinkle with the parsley and serve at once.

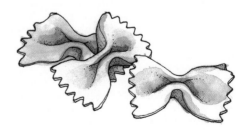

Penne al sugo di maiale e acciughe

{ Penne with roast pork juices and anchovy sauce }

Serves 4

1kg/2lb 4oz joint of pork
shoulder or belly, boned
and firmly tied

50g/1¾oz/4 tbsp unsalted
butter

4 tbsp olive oil

1 garlic clove, chopped

6 anchovy fillets, chopped

needles from a 20cm/8 inch
sprig of fresh rosemary

grated rind and juice of
1 unwaxed lemon

150ml/5fl oz/⅔ cup dry
white wine

salt and freshly ground
black pepper

150ml/5fl oz/⅔ cup meat
stock or water, heated

350g/12oz penne

1 tbsp Italian 00 flour

2 tbsp chopped flat-leaf
parsley

freshly grated Parmesan
cheese

This recipe will provide two dishes: this pasta dish, and a well-flavoured piece of pork to have cold the next day. The cold pork is delicious with any sort of salad: green, potato, green bean or, especially, fennel.

Preheat the oven to 180°C/350°F/gas mark 4.

In a heavy-bottomed casserole big enough to hold the meat comfortably, heat half the butter and the oil. Add the garlic, anchovy fillets and rosemary and fry for a few minutes, mashing the anchovies with a fork.

Add the pork and brown it on all sides. Add the lemon juice and rind, the wine and some salt and pepper. Cook for a few minutes and then pour in the heated stock or water. Mix well, cover the pan with a lid and place it in the oven. Cook for about 1½–2 hours, until the meat is very tender.

Remove the meat from the casserole and set it aside for another meal. Pour the liquid into a measuring jug. You need about 250ml/9fl oz/1 cup for the sauce: if there is more, keep it to serve, defatted, with the meat; if less, add a little water. Return the liquid to the casserole and bring to the boil. Mix in the flour and cook for 2–3 minutes, scraping the bottom of the pan to release all the lovely bits stuck to it. If necessary, add a little hot water.

Cook the pasta in boiling salted water.

Put the remaining butter in a serving bowl and warm in the oven, which is still warm from the cooking of the meat. When the pasta is ready, drain it and turn it into the warmed bowl. Mix thoroughly to coat it with the melted butter and then mix in all the lovely meat juices. Sprinkle with the parsley and serve with Parmesan.

Linguine con 'nduja

{ Linguine with 'nduja and tomato sauce }

Serves 4

4 tbsp olive oil, or 30g/1oz
  lardo (Italian cured pork
  back fat)

1 large red onion,
  very thinly sliced

200g/7oz 'nduja,
  roughly cubed

500ml/18fl oz/2¼ cups
  passata (strained tomatoes)

salt

350g/12oz linguine

'Nduja, or *'ndugghia*, is a fiery salame made in Calabria, near Tropea – which is also the birthplace of the best red onions. Being very hot, it is the perfect sausage for a pasta ragù when combined with the sweetness of tomatoes.

'Nduja is now available in many supermarkets and it has recently become the 'in' food par excellence. I certainly do not think food should be fashionable and would not write this recipe just for the sake of it; I write it because it is a sauce of delicious flavour and utter simplicity.

Heat the oil or lardo in a large frying pan and add the onion. Sauté for 7–8 minutes, until the onion is soft, stirring very frequently.

Chuck the 'nduja into the frying pan and sauté for about 4 minutes. Pour in the passata and season with salt to taste. Cook for 10 minutes.

While the sauce is cooking, cook the linguine in boiling salted water. Drain and turn it into the frying pan. Stir-fry for a couple of minutes, using two forks to lift the linguine high so that all the strands get coated with the sauce. Serve at once.

No cheese is served with this sauce in Calabria, but if you want to serve it, pecorino would be far better than Parmesan.

Tagliatelle con gulasch alla triestina

{ Tagliatelle with goulash }

Serves 4

300g/10½oz dried egg
tagliatelle, or homemade
tagliatelle (pages 58–61)
made with 200g/7oz Italian
00 flour and 2 eggs

6 tbsp vegetable oil

300g/10½oz onions (about
3 onions), chopped

2 large red peppers, cut into
thin strips

100g/3½oz smoked pancetta,
cubed

3 best-quality pork sausages,
cut into chunks

750g/1lb 10oz rindless pork
belly, cut into cubes

1–2 tbsp strong paprika,
depending on strength

1 tbsp tomato purée (paste)

1 tbsp Italian 00 flour

200ml/7fl oz/generous ¾ cup
red wine

250ml/9fl oz/1 cup beef
stock

salt and freshly ground
black pepper

juice of ½ an unwaxed lemon
and 1 tsp of the grated rind

50g/1¾oz/4 tbsp unsalted
butter

This goulash from Trieste is as full-flavoured and appetizing as its more famous cousin from Hungary. It is an easily made dish, always served as a main course, which, apart from the cooking of the tagliatelle, can all be prepared in advance. The pasta here is an accompaniment to the meat and should be served alongside it, not mixed in as for a ragù.

If you are making the pasta at home, follow the instructions on pages 58–61.

Preheat the oven to 180°C/350°F/gas mark 4.

Heat half the oil in a sauté pan, add the onions and fry them gently for 5 minutes. Throw in the peppers and cook for 5 minutes, stirring very frequently. Remove the pan from the heat and set aside.

Heat the remaining oil in a heavy-bottomed casserole, add the pancetta and fry until crisp. Using a slotted spoon, remove the pancetta to a plate and chuck in the sausages and the pork. Brown well on all sides for about 5–6 minutes and then stir in 1 tablespoon of the paprika, the tomato purée and flour. Cook for 2 minutes, stirring all the time. Pour in the wine and boil briskly to partly evaporate. Add the stock, salt and pepper to taste and the lemon rind and juice. Taste and add more paprika if needed. Put the casserole in the oven and cook for about 1 hour, or until the pork is tender.

Cook the tagliatelle in boiling salted water, keeping in mind that homemade tagliatelle will be ready in 2 minutes. Drain and turn into a warmed bowl. Dress immediately with the butter and a few tablespoons of the sauce and serve alongside the goulash.

Pappardelle con la lepre

{ Pappardelle with hare }

Serves 6

homemade pappardelle
(pages 58–61) made with
300g/10½oz Italian 00 flour
and 3 eggs, or 400g/14oz
dried egg pappardelle or
reginette

2 tbsp olive oil

100g/3½oz/scant ½ cup
unsalted butter

100g/3½oz unsmoked
pancetta, cubed

1 small onion, finely chopped

1 carrot, finely chopped

1 celery stalk, finely chopped

2 garlic cloves,
finely chopped

needles from a sprig of
rosemary

the back legs of a hare

2 tsp Italian 00 flour

200ml/7fl oz/generous ¾ cup
red wine

200ml/7fl oz/generous ¾ cup
meat stock, or more
if necessary

½ tsp ground cinnamon

grated nutmeg (about ¼ of
a nutmeg)

salt and freshly ground
black pepper

4 heaped tbsp sour cream

3 tbsp chopped fresh parsley

The Tuscans are Italy's keenest hunters. On the first day of the shooting season the whole region explodes. Pheasants, hares and even larks and thrushes become victims of this passion, the only good result of which is superb game recipes.

In this recipe only the hare's back legs are used. Keep the saddle and front legs for another meal; hare freezes very well. Pappardelle, one of the two traditional Tuscan pasta shapes, are very broad noodles (about 3cm/1¼ inches wide), sometimes with ruffled edges. The rolled-out pasta dough is cut with a fluted pastry wheel.

If you are making the pasta at home, follow the instructions on pages 58–61.

In a large, heavy-bottomed saucepan heat the oil and half of the butter and sauté the pancetta for 1–2 minutes. Add the onion and cook for a few minutes, until it is translucent. Add the carrot, celery, garlic and rosemary and sauté for 10 minutes.

Lightly coat the hare legs with the flour, add to the pan and cook until brown on all sides. Pour in the wine, turn up the heat, and cook until the liquid has reduced by half. Add the stock, cinnamon, nutmeg, salt and pepper. Turn the heat down and cook, covered, for a good hour, or until you can easily pierce the thickest part of the hare drumstick with the point of a knife. Add a little more stock if the sauce gets too dry.

Remove the hare from the pan. Cut all the meat off the bones and cut it into small pieces. Return the meat to the sauce, mix in the sour cream and keep hot.

Cook the pappardelle in boiling salted water and drain, reserving a cupful of the water. Turn the pasta into a warmed bowl and dress immediately with the remaining butter. Spoon the sauce over the mound of pappardelle, sprinkle with the parsley and serve at once.

Pappardelle alla maceratese

{ Pappardelle with pork, anchovy fillets and tomato sauce }

Serves 4–6

homemade pappardelle
(pages 58–61) made with
300g/10½oz Italian 00 flour
and 3 eggs, or 400g/14oz
dried egg pappardelle or
reginette

5 tbsp olive oil

50g/1¾oz unsmoked
pancetta, cubed

1 onion, chopped

1 celery stalk, chopped

350g/12oz pork, coarsely
minced (ground)

150ml/5fl oz/⅔ cup dry
white wine

4 anchovy fillets, mashed, or
2 salted anchovies, cleaned
and rinsed and mashed

250g/9oz/1 cup plain tomato
sauce (page 72)

salt and freshly ground
black pepper

2 tbsp olio santo (page 64)

freshly grated pecorino or
Parmesan cheese, to serve

Pappardelle, the Tuscan pasta, are also popular in Le Marche, the region to the east of Tuscany. They are broad noodles with ruffled edges, cut with a fluted pastry wheel from a *sfoglia* that has been allowed to dry only briefly.

If you are making the pasta at home, follow the instructions on pages 58–61.

Heat the oil in a frying pan and gently fry the pancetta for 1–2 minutes. Add the onion and celery and sauté for 5 minutes and then turn up the heat, throw in the meat and brown quickly all over. Pour in the wine and reduce over high heat. Turn the heat down, add the anchovy fillets and cook for 2–3 minutes, squashing them against the pan.

Spoon in the tomato sauce, season with salt and pepper and simmer, covered, for about 30 minutes, adding a little warm water if the sauce becomes too dry.

Cook the pappardelle in boiling salted water. Drain, turn them into a warmed serving bowl, and pour over the olio santo. Mix well and then mix in the pork ragù. Serve with grated cheese.

Bucatini all'amatriciana

{ Bucatini with pancetta }

Serves 4

1 tbsp olive oil

350g/12oz unsmoked
pancetta or *guanciale*, cubed

1 onion, very finely chopped

1 garlic clove,
very finely chopped

400g/14oz canned chopped
tomatoes, with some of the
juice discarded

½ tsp crushed dried chillies

250ml/9fl oz/½ cup dry
white wine

salt and freshly ground
black pepper

350g/12oz bucatini

6 tbsp freshly grated
pecorino cheese, plus extra
to serve

In Abruzzo and Lazio, where this recipe originates, the sauce is made with *guanciale*, cured pig's jowl. This delicious pork product is not easily available outside Italy, but pancetta is a good substitute. If you can get *guanciale*, cut the slices into 5cm/2 inch-long sticks and then into 2cm/¾ inch cubes.

Heat the oil in a large frying pan, throw in the pancetta and fry until crisp and brown. Using a slotted spoon, remove the pancetta to a plate. Add the onion to the pan and sauté for about 7 minutes. Throw in the garlic, tomatoes and chilli and sauté gently for 5 minutes. Splash with the wine and let it bubble away to reduce by half. Put the pancetta back into the pan, add some salt and pepper and simmer for about 15 minutes. Taste and adjust the seasoning.

While the sauce is cooking, cook the bucatini in boiling salted water. Drain and turn it into the frying pan. Stir-fry for 2 minutes, using two forks to lift the strands high so that they all get coated in the sauce. Mix in 6 tablespoons of pecorino and serve extra cheese on the side.

Maccheroni alla chitarra

{ Macaroni with lamb ragù }

Serves 4

50g/1¾oz lardo or unsmoked
   pancetta, cut into
   small cubes

300g/10½oz lamb fillet,
   trimmed and cubed

½–1 tsp crushed dried
   chillies, to taste

1 garlic clove, crushed

1 tbsp dried oregano

salt and freshly ground
   black pepper

4 tbsp olive oil

125g/4½oz brown
   mushrooms, chopped

1 small onion, chopped

4 tbsp red wine

3 tbsp red wine vinegar

1 tbsp Italian 00 flour

2 tbsp tomato purée (paste)

350g/12oz dried tonnarelli
   or bucatini

1 tbsp chopped fresh parsley

This is one of the oldest dishes of Abruzzo and Molise in southern Italy. The pasta dough is made with durum wheat semolina and water and rolled out, not too thinly, then pressed through wires stretched across a wooden frame – the *chitarra* (guitar). The resulting strands, called tonnarelli, are like square spaghetti. The recipe name, 'maccheroni alla chitarra', dates back to the time when macaroni was used as a general term for pasta, as it still is in some parts of Italy.

The traditional sauces for this pasta are the lamb ragù below or a sauce similar to amatriciana (page 97) but even fiercer. *Lardo* – nothing like the English lard – is pork back fat, salt-cured in a similar way to bacon. It can sometimes be found in Italian delis, or it can be bought online.

Locally the pasta is served first, and the meat is served as a second course accompanied by some green vegetables, or at a different meal. But you could serve it with the pasta on the same dish for a very nourishing one-dish meal.

Heat the lardo or pancetta in a frying pan and when it begins to fizzle throw in the lamb and fry for 5 minutes, stirring the whole time. Add the chilli, garlic, oregano and a little salt and fry for 1 minute. Using a slotted spoon, lift the meat out of the pan and set aside.

Add the oil to the pan and when the oil is hot, throw in the mushrooms and sauté for 5 minutes, stirring frequently. Season with salt and a little pepper and continue cooking fast for 2 minutes. Lift out the mushrooms and set aside with the lamb.

Now put the onion into the pan and sauté until golden. Pour in the wine and the vinegar, and boil briskly until nearly all the liquid has evaporated.

Mix in the flour and the tomato purée and cook for 2 minutes, stirring constantly. Return the lamb and the mushrooms to the pan and cook over very low heat until the lamb is tender, about 20 minutes. Taste and adjust seasoning.

When the lamb is ready, cook the pasta in plenty of boiling salted water. Drain and turn into a warmed bowl. Mix in a little of the sauce liquid and then spoon the rest of the sauce with all the meat over the top. Sprinkle with the parsley and serve at once.

Malloreddus al ragù d'agnello

{ Malloreddus with lamb ragù and mint }

Serves 4

2 pinches of saffron strands

4 tbsp olive oil

1 garlic clove, crushed

350g/12oz lamb fillet, cut
  into small cubes

150ml/5fl oz/⅔ cup red wine

400g/14oz canned chopped
  tomatoes

1 tbsp tomato purée (paste)

salt and freshly ground
  black pepper

350g/12oz gnocchetti sardi

30g/1oz/2 tbsp unsalted
  butter

75g/2¾oz pecorino cheese,
  grated

2 tbsp coarsely chopped
  fresh mint

Malloreddus, also called gnocchetti sardi, are one of the two traditional pastas of Sardinia; they are made with a dough of durum wheat semolina and water to which saffron is added. The dough is shaped into sticks, cut into short pieces and these little pieces are pressed through a special wicker basket. Homemade malloreddus are found only in Sardinia and they are one of the best local specialities. However, dried gnocchetti sardi are industrially made and are widely available. They are traditionally dressed with a sausage and tomato sauce flavoured with saffron, or with this lamb ragù, which contains, besides saffron, also mint, a herb not often used in Italian cooking.

Put the saffron strands in a small cup, add 3–4 tablespoons of hot water and set aside to soak.

Heat the oil in a large frying pan, add the garlic and fry for 1 minute. Add the meat and brown well on all sides. Pour in the wine and reduce over high heat for 2–3 minutes. Add the tomatoes, tomato purée and salt and pepper to taste. Stir in the saffron strands with their liquid and simmer, uncovered, for about 45 minutes, until the lamb is very tender. If the sauce becomes too dry, add a little warm water.

Cook the pasta in boiling salted water, drain, and turn it into a warmed bowl. Toss with the butter, cover with the meat sauce and sprinkle with half of the cheese and all of the mint. Mix thoroughly and serve at once, with the rest of the cheese on the side.

Tortiglioni con pollo al curry

{ Tortiglioni with curried chicken }

Serves 6

60g/2¼oz/4 tbsp unsalted
  butter

3 banana shallots,
  thinly sliced

350g/12oz cooked chicken,
  cut into cubes

2 tsp curry powder, or more
  if desired

4 tbsp dry sherry

salt

2 heaped tbsp sour cream

400g/14oz tortiglioni

2 tbsp olive oil

2 tbsp chopped fresh
  coriander (cilantro)

In this Italy-meets-India recipe I use ready-made curry powder, simply because you need so little and the emphasis is on the pasta. But of course you can make your own curry powder, and the sauce might be even nicer, although that would be quite difficult. This is an ideal way to use leftover roast chicken or turkey.

Heat the butter in a sauté pan and when the foam begins to subside, add the shallots and cook for about 5 minutes, adding a little hot water to prevent them from sticking. Throw in the chicken and sauté for 1–2 minutes, then add the curry powder and cook for 2 minutes, stirring the whole time and adding a little hot water if the sauce gets too dry.

Pour in the sherry and reduce over high heat for a minute or two, then turn the heat down and cook, covered, for 5 minutes. Season with salt to taste, add the sour cream and mix thoroughly.

While the sauce is cooking, cook the pasta in boiling salted water. Drain the pasta and turn it into a warmed bowl. Dress immediately with the oil and then mix in some of the curry sauce. Spoon the chicken and the remaining sauce over the top, sprinkle with the coriander and serve at once.

Penne in salsa di pollo

{ Penne with chicken sauce }

Serves 4

1 small chicken, about
   1.3kg/3lb

1 small onion, chopped

1 small carrot, chopped

1 small celery stalk, chopped

250ml/9fl oz/1 cup red or
   dry white wine

125ml4fl oz/½ cup olive oil

salt and freshly ground
   black pepper

350g/12oz penne or rigatoni

30g/1oz/2 tbsp unsalted
   butter

freshly grated Parmesan
   cheese, to serve

The chicken breast, delicious cooked this way, is served as a separate course, hot or cold. The juices from cooking the chicken are used to make the sauce for the pasta.

Preheat the oven to 190°C/375°F/gas mark 5.

Put the chicken in an oval flameproof lidded casserole, into which it will just fit. Add all the vegetables, wine, oil, salt and pepper and about 100ml/3½fl oz/ scant ½ cup of water. Cover the casserole, put it in the oven and cook for about 1½ hours, or until the chicken is cooked. Test by pushing the point of a small knife into a thigh; the liquid running out should be clear.

Remove the casserole from the oven, place it on the heat and cook over high heat to reduce the liquid, while turning the chicken over on all sides to brown. Lift the bird out and place on a board. If the cooking juices are too liquid, boil fast to reduce and thicken slightly.

Cook the pasta in boiling salted water. While the pasta is cooking, remove all the meat from the chicken thighs and drumsticks and cut into small pieces. (Keep the breasts for another meal.) Mix the diced meat into the chicken cooking juices.

When the pasta is ready, drain and turn into a warmed bowl. Toss immediately with the butter and then spoon the sauce over it and serve at once, with a bowl of grated Parmesan on the side.

Maccheroncini al fagiano

{ Maccheroncini with pheasant sauce }

Serves 4–6

1 pheasant, preferably
  a hen bird

125g/4½oz/generous ½ cup
  unsalted butter

125g/4½oz unsmoked
  pancetta, cubed

125ml/4fl oz/½ cup brandy

salt and freshly ground
  black pepper

350g/12oz macaroni

1 onion, chopped

1 celery stalk, chopped

a grating of nutmeg

250ml/9fl oz/1 cup red wine

125ml/4fl oz/½ cup double
  (heavy) cream

freshly grated Parmesan
  cheese, to serve (optional)

An all-in-one dish, perfect for an autumn supper.

In a saucepan into which the pheasant will just fit, heat half the butter. Add the pancetta and fry until crisp. Add the bird and brown lightly on all sides. Pour in the brandy, boil very briskly for about 1 minute, and then season with salt and pepper. Reduce the heat, cover the pan and simmer for about 45 minutes, turning the bird over two or three times, until it is cooked.

Lift the bird out of the pan and place on a board. When it is cool enough to handle, remove all the meat from the bones and chop the meat into small pieces.

Cook the pasta in boiling salted water. While the pasta is cooking, heat the remaining butter in a sauté pan, add the onion and celery and sauté for about 7–8 minutes. Add the pheasant meat, the nutmeg and salt and pepper and mix well. Pour in the wine and boil briskly to reduce. If the sauce appears dry, add a little water and simmer, covered, for about 5 minutes.

When the pasta is ready, drain and turn into a warmed bowl. Mix in the cream and then add all the delicious pheasant sauce and mix well. Serve at once and, if you like, hand around a bowl of grated Parmesan.

Insalata di ruote e pollo

{ Ruote and chicken salad }

Serves 4

300g/10½oz ruote or ditali

5 tbsp olive oil

350g/12oz cold roast
chicken, cut into strips

4 cornichons, sliced

2 tbsp chopped fresh parsley

½ garlic clove, finely chopped

1 tbsp balsamic vinegar

a few drops each of Tabasco
and Worcestershire sauce

salt and freshly ground
black pepper

This is an excellent way to finish off the remains of the roasted chicken from Sunday lunch. It is also one of the best cold pasta dishes I know.

Cook and drain the pasta. Turn it into a large mixing bowl, toss with 2 tablespoons of the olive oil, and leave to cool.

In another bowl mix together the chicken, cornichons, parsley and garlic. Add the vinegar and the remaining oil, then add Tabasco and Worcester sauces to taste, and season with salt and pepper. Spoon the dressing over the pasta. Mix well and serve at room temperature.

Fish

Pasta and seafood are a marriage made in heaven.
Just think of eating a dish of spaghetti with clams
or with scallops and you really are in heaven,
especially if you are eating it by the sea on the
Zattere in Venice or at Santa Lucia in Naples.

Some of these recipes are for typical Italian
first courses, while others are quite substantial
dishes – spaghetti with squid and pesto or ziti with
haddock, for example, are more of a
one-dish meal.

Pasta al tonno in bianco

{ Pasta with tuna }

Serves 4

350g/12oz gomiti

150ml/5fl oz/⅔ cup extra
virgin olive oil

1 garlic clove, finely sliced

4 tbsp chopped flat-leaf
parsley

4 tbsp capers

grated rind of ½ unwaxed
lemon

300g/10½oz best-quality
tuna preserved in olive oil,
drained and crumbled

salt and freshly ground
black pepper

This is one of the many recipes for pasta with tuna. It is called '*in bianco*', meaning 'white', because it doesn't contain tomatoes. It was created by my daughter and I was so impressed that I had to pass it on, hoping you will like it. It is ideal to dress a bowl of gomiti or fusilli.

Cook the pasta in boiling salted water.

While the pasta is cooking, heat half the oil in a large frying pan and, when hot, add the garlic, half the parsley, the capers and lemon rind. Cook for a minute or two and then stir in the tuna, salt and pepper. Cook for a further 2 minutes, breaking up the tuna as much as you can with a fork.

When the pasta is ready, drain and transfer it to the frying pan. Add the remaining oil and stir-fry for 1–2 minutes. Sprinkle with the remaining parsley and serve at once.

Linguine in salsa di tonno

{ Linguine in tuna sauce }

Serves 4

6 tbsp extra virgin olive oil

1 small onion, finely chopped

2 garlic cloves, finely
chopped

500g/1lb 2oz fresh tomatoes,
peeled, seeded and chopped

4 tbsp capers

[continues opposite]

125g/4½oz/¾ cup pitted

Tinned tuna can be horrid. I advise you to buy albacore tuna in chunks, packed in olive oil; not cheap, but well worth the difference in price from the common or garden tuna.

Heat 4 tablespoons of the oil in a sauté pan, add the onion and sauté until translucent. Add the garlic and the tomatoes and cook for 5 minutes over high heat. Turn the heat down and add the capers, olives and celery. Simmer for 10 minutes and then add the tuna and cook gently for about 2 minutes. Taste and add salt if necessary, and plenty of pepper.

black olives

1 small celery stalk, very
finely chopped

200g/7oz canned tuna,
drained and shredded

salt and freshly ground
black pepper

350g/12oz linguine

a dozen fresh basil leaves,
torn into pieces

While the sauce is cooking, cook the pasta in boiling salted water. Drain and turn it into a serving bowl and toss immediately with the remaining oil. Cover with the sauce and sprinkle the basil leaves. No cheese is needed.

Spaghettini con le cappe sante

{ Spaghettini with scallops }

Serves 4

10–12 fresh scallops with
their corals

125ml/4fl oz/½ cup extra
virgin olive oil

50g/1¾oz/½ cup dried white
breadcrumbs

350g/12oz spaghettini (thin
spaghetti)

2 garlic cloves, finely
chopped

2 tbsp chopped flat-leaf
parsley

2 tbsp fresh thyme leaves

1 tsp crushed dried chillies

4 tbsp dry vermouth

Originally from Venice, where the scallops (*canestrelli*) are small and full of flavour, this sauce works very well with the large Atlantic scallops. It needs careful timing so that both the pasta and the scallops are ready at the same time.

Detach the corals from the scallops and slice the white part into three or four slices.

Heat 2 tablespoons of the oil in a large frying pan, add the breadcrumbs and fry for about 3 minutes, stirring frequently, until golden. Using a slotted spoon, scoop out the crumbs from the oil and set aside.

Drop the spaghettini into a pan of boiling salted water.

Heat half the remaining oil in the frying pan, add the garlic, parsley, thyme and chilli and cook for about 2 minutes.

When the pasta is nearly ready, throw the white part of the scallops into the frying pan and sauté for 30 seconds. Now add the coral and the vermouth and boil briskly for no more than 1 minute. Drain the spaghettini and turn into the frying pan. Pour over the remaining oil and stir-fry for 1 minute. Serve at once.

Fusilli alla Mafia

{ Fusilli with anchovies and black olives }

Serves 4

350g/12oz fusilli

5 tbsp extra virgin olive oil

3 salted anchovies, cleaned,
  rinsed and chopped, or
  6 anchovy fillets, drained
  and chopped

2 garlic cloves, finely
  chopped

the rind of 1 unwaxed lemon,
  cut into thin strips

¼ tsp crushed dried chillies

60g/2¼oz/⅓ cup black
  olives, pitted and cut into
  small strips

4 tbsp chopped flat-leaf
  parsley

salt

freshly grated pecorino
  cheese

This sauce derives its name from its Sicilian origin, although it is quite popular all over southern Italy.

Drop the fusilli into a pan of boiling salted water.

Heat the oil in a large frying pan. When the oil is hot add the anchovies, and mash them with a fork as they cook. Add the garlic, lemon rind, chilli, olives, parsley and a pinch or two of salt. Mix thoroughly and cook for 2–3 minutes.

When the pasta is ready, drain and transfer it to the frying pan and cook for 2 minutes, stirring constantly. Serve with a bowl of grated pecorino.

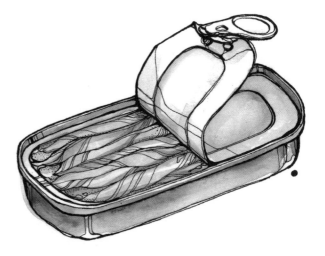

Ziti con filetti di nasello

{ Ziti with haddock fillets }

Serves 4–6

350g/12oz haddock fillets

100ml/3½fl oz/scant ½ cup
extra virgin olive oil

1 garlic clove, finely chopped

2 salted anchovies, cleaned
and rinsed, or 4 anchovy
fillets, drained

½–1 tsp crushed dried
chillies, to taste

500g/1lb 2oz fresh tomatoes,
peeled and seeded, or
canned plum tomatoes

salt

400g/14oz ziti

a few sprigs of parsley,
chopped

I like the substantial body of the ziti – a thick, long, hollow pasta – for this substantial pasta dish. If haddock is not available, you could use another firm white fish such as cod, hake or pollack.

Skin the haddock and cut it into small pieces.

Heat half the oil in a large frying pan, add the garlic and the anchovies and cook for a couple of minutes, mashing the anchovies to a paste against the bottom of the pan. Add the haddock and the chilli and sauté for a minute or two, turning the fish over and over.

Blitz the tomatoes in a food processor and add to the sauce together with a pinch of salt. Cook over moderate heat for 10 minutes. Taste and adjust the seasoning.

While the sauce is cooking, cook the pasta in boiling salted water. Drain and toss immediately with the remaining oil. Divide the ziti among four warmed plates and spoon the fish and its sauce over the pasta. Sprinkle with the parsley and serve at once.

Linguine con salsa di gamberetti e piselli

{ Linguine with prawns and peas }

Serves 4

250g/9oz/1¾ cups shelled
  peas or frozen petits pois,
  thawed

40g/1½oz/3 tbsp unsalted
  butter

3 tbsp olive oil

2 shallots, grated

250g/9oz fresh peeled
  prawns (shrimp) or frozen
  prawns, thawed

2 tbsp dry sherry

salt and freshly ground
  black pepper

350g/12oz linguine

125ml/4fl oz/½ cup double
  (heavy) cream

3–4 drops green Tabasco
  sauce

freshly grated Parmesan, to
  serve (optional)

For this recipe you can use cooked peeled prawns to save time. It is a good recipe to make if you have a pack of them in the freezer.

If you are using fresh peas, cook them until barely tender by simmering them, covered, in 125ml/4fl oz/½ cup water with a third of the butter for about 5 minutes. If you are using frozen peas, boil them for about 1 minute.

Heat the remaining butter and the oil in a large frying pan. Add the shallots and cook for 2–3 minutes, stirring frequently. Add the prawns and the peas, and after a minute or two, pour in the sherry. Cook over high heat for 2 minutes, stirring constantly. Season with salt and pepper to taste. If the pasta is not ready, remove the pan from the heat, or the prawns will be overcooked.

While the sauce is cooking, drop the pasta into a pan of boiling salted water.

Just before you drain the linguine, mix the cream and the Tabasco into the sauce.

Drain the pasta, reserving a cupful of the water. Transfer the pasta to the frying pan with the sauce, mix well and cook for no longer than 1 minute, adding a little of the reserved pasta water to loosen the sauce if necessary. Serve at once. This is one of the few dishes of pasta with fish with which you can serve some grated Parmesan.

Spaghetti al caviale

{ Spaghetti with caviar }

Serves 4

350g/12oz spaghetti or other
long pasta strands

50g/1¾oz/4 tbsp unsalted
butter

12 fresh chives, snipped

4 tbsp mascarpone cheese

50–60g/about 2oz caviar or
black lumpfish roe

salt and freshly ground
black pepper

juice of ½ lemon

This sauce is very good, and is easy and quick to make. You don't need to use
real caviar, of course; lumpfish roe will do, but buy a good brand.

Drop the spaghetti into a pan of boiling salted water.

Heat the butter in a large frying pan, add the chives and cook for a couple of
minutes. Mix in the mascarpone and continue cooking for a couple of minutes.
Add the lumpfish roe and cook for 1 minute, stirring constantly and adding a
little of the pasta cooking water if the sauce gets too dry.

When the pasta is ready, drain, and turn it into the frying pan. Taste and add
a little salt if necessary, and plenty of pepper. Add the lemon juice, mix well and
serve at once.

Chifferi con i pepperoni arrostiti

{ Elbow macaroni with anchovies and peppers }

Serves 4

2 yellow and/or red peppers

6 tbsp extra virgin olive oil

3 salted anchovies, cleaned
  and rinsed, or 6 anchovy
  fillets, drained, pounded to
  a paste

1 garlic clove, crushed

1 tsp French mustard

250g/9oz fresh tomatoes,
  peeled, seeded and chopped

salt

350g/12oz elbow macaroni
  or other short pasta

2 tbsp fresh basil leaves, torn
  into pieces

The name of this pasta shape, chifferi, derives from the Austrian biscuit, *kipferl*. They are short, ridged, half moon shapes, which I have chosen for this salad for no other reason than that they are pretty. Ditali or penne would also be good here.

Put the peppers on a direct flame or under the grill and roast until the outer skin is black and blistered. Turn the peppers around and continue roasting them until the skin is charred on all sides. When they are cool, quarter and peel the peppers carefully, discarding the seeds and the ribs. Cut them vertically into thin strips. This can be done in advance; put the pepper strips into a container and pour over a tablespoon of extra virgin olive oil. They keep very well in the fridge for 4–5 days.

In a large bowl, mix together the oil, mashed anchovies, garlic, mustard, peppers and tomatoes. Add salt to taste and beat well.

Cook the pasta in boiling salted water. Drain and turn it into the bowl with the other ingredients. Mix thoroughly. Leave the pasta to cool for about 1 hour. Just before serving, sprinkle with the basil.

Spaghetti con le seppie

{ Spaghetti with cuttlefish }

Serves 6

500g/1lb 2oz cuttlefish
  or squid

6 tbsp extra virgin olive oil

1 onion, finely chopped

2 garlic cloves,
  finely chopped

250g/9oz fresh tomatoes,
  peeled and seeded, or
  canned plum tomatoes

150ml/5fl oz/⅔ cup red or
  dry white wine

½ tsp crushed dried chillies

salt and freshly ground
  black pepper

350g/12oz spaghetti

3 tbsp chopped flat-leaf
  parsley

You can use squid, although cuttlefish are better, having a more distinctive flavour. The cuttlefish should be small. I hope you have an obliging fishmonger who will clean them for you; otherwise, follow my instructions at the beginning of the recipe. It is not a difficult job, only very messy.

To clean the cuttlefish (or squid), hold the body sac in one hand and with the other hand pull off the tentacles. As you pull, the internal organs should all come out of the sac. Reserve the tentacles and the body and discard the entrails. Remove the bone (with squid, this is thin and clear) from the sac and peel off as much as you can of the thin dark skin covering the body sac. Wash thoroughly both sac and tentacles and pat dry with kitchen paper. Cut the tentacles into small pieces and the body into thin short strips.

Heat 4 tablespoons of the oil in a sauté pan and sauté the onion until soft. Press the onion against the sides of the pan with a wooden spoon to release the juices. Add the garlic and the tomatoes and cook over moderately high heat for 10 minutes, stirring frequently.

Add the tentacles and cook for 2 minutes, then add the body strips and cook for a further 3 minutes, stirring the whole time. Pour in the wine and boil rapidly for 2 minutes. Season with the chilli, salt and pepper. Turn down the heat and cook over low heat until the cuttlefish or squid are tender, usually about 40 minutes, but it depends on their size.

Some 15 minutes before the cuttlefish is tender, bring a large pan of water to the boil for the spaghetti. Add 1½–2 tablespoons of salt and then add the spaghetti to the rapidly boiling water. When the spaghetti is ready, drain and turn it into a large warmed bowl, toss with the remaining oil and then spoon the sauce and the cuttlefish over the top. Sprinkle with the parsley and serve. No cheese is needed.

Spaghetti con le seppie al nero
Spaghetti with cuttlefish ink

This variation of the sauce contains the ink from the cuttlefish and has no tomatoes. It has a brilliant blue-black colour and a delicious fishy taste. You will find the ink sac among the entrails when you pull them out – ask your fishmonger to keep it if he or she is cleaning the cuttlefish for you. Set aside the ink in a cup.

Proceed as for the preceding recipe, but use a small onion; omit the tomatoes and cook the garlic for just 1–2 minutes before adding the tentacles; and add the ink squeezed from the ink sacs before adding the wine. This will serve 5–6.

Spaghetti e cozze al sugo di pomodoro

{ *Spaghetti with mussels and tomatoes* }

Serves 4

1kg/2lb 4oz fresh live
  mussels in their shells

4 tbsp extra virgin olive oil

2 garlic cloves,
  finely chopped

500g/1lb 2oz fresh tomatoes,
  peeled and seeded, or
  canned plum tomatoes

salt and freshly ground
  black pepper

350g/12oz spaghetti

2 tbsp chopped flat-leaf
  parsley

Only buy mussels when you can see that most of the shells are tightly closed.

To clean the mussels, put them in a sink full of cold water and go through them thoroughly; discard any mussels that remain open after you tap them on a hard surface, and any broken shells. Scrub the mussels thoroughly with a hard brush, scraping off any barnacles with a knife. Put them back in the sink, cover with fresh cold water and leave for about 10 minutes to allow any sand to sink to the bottom, then drain them.

Put the cleaned mussels in a large shallow pan. Cover and cook over high heat until the mussels open, turning them over occasionally; this will take about 4 minutes. Remove the meat from the shells and discard the shells. Discard any shells that remain closed. Strain the liquid that remains at the bottom of the pan through a fine sieve into another pan and reduce it over high heat. You should have about 250ml/9fl oz/1 cup left.

Heat the oil and garlic in a large frying pan. Add the tomatoes (if you are using canned tomatoes, discard the juice) and cook, uncovered, over high heat for 5 minutes. Add 150ml/5fl oz/⅔ cup of the mussel liquid. Taste and adjust the seasoning.

Cook the spaghetti in boiling salted water. Drain, turn it into the frying pan and stir-fry for 1 minute. Add the mussels and cook for 2–3 minutes, adding a little more of the mussel liquid. Sprinkle with the parsley and serve at once.

Linguine con guance di coda di rospo

{ Linguine with monkfish cheeks, tomatoes, chilli and lemon }

Serves 4

300g/10½oz monkfish
  cheeks

350g/12oz linguine

6 tbsp extra virgin olive oil

2 garlic cloves, chopped

4 anchovy fillets, chopped

2 tbsp chopped fresh oregano
  or marjoram

½ tsp crushed dried chillies

grated rind of ½ unwaxed
  lemon and a few drops of
  the juice

6 cherry tomatoes, peeled
  and chopped

salt

2 tbsp capers

Monkfish cheeks are often seen on the fishmonger's counter and they should never be ignored. They can be coated in egg and breadcrumbs and fried, or used to make this sauce.

Remove any skin from the monkfish and cut the fish into 2cm/¾ inch cubes.

Cook the linguine in boiling salted water.

While the pasta is cooking, heat 4 tablespoons of the oil in a large frying pan, add the garlic, anchovy fillets, oregano, chilli and lemon rind and fry for 1 minute, stirring constantly. Add the tomatoes, fry for 3–4 minutes and then throw in the monkfish and sauté for 3 minutes. Squeeze in a few drops of lemon juice and season with salt. If the pasta is not ready, remove the pan from the heat, or the monkfish will become dry.

When the pasta is ready, drain and turn it into the frying pan. Add the capers and the remaining oil and stir-fry for 2–3 minutes. Serve at once. No Parmesan is needed for this sauce.

Spaghetti in bianco con le vongole

{ Spaghetti with clams }

Serves 4

1kg/2lb 4oz fresh live clams
    in their shells

6 tbsp dry white wine

350g/12oz spaghetti

5 tbsp olive oil

3 garlic cloves,
    finely chopped

grated rind of ½ unwaxed
    lemon

salt

¼ tsp crushed dried chillies

½ tbsp dried oregano
    (optional)

3 tbsp chopped flat-leaf
    parsley

The only clams I use are palourdes – also known as carpet shells or Manila clams – which in Italian are called *vongole verace* ('true clams'). These are larger than the common variety of clams, have grey shells marked with a dark line, and have a far superior flavour.

Soak the clams in a sink full of cold water and go through them carefully; throw away any that remain open after you tap them on a hard surface, and any with a cracked shell.

Rinse the clams in fresh cold water and then put them in a large sauté pan. Pour in the wine, cover the pan and cook over high heat until the clams open, about 3–4 minutes. Shake the pan occasionally so that they all get the same amount of heat from the bottom of the pan. Set aside about 20 clams in their shells and remove the meat from the shells of all the remaining clams. Reserve the clam cooking liquid in the pan.

Drop the spaghetti into a pan of boiling salted water.

While the pasta is cooking, heat the oil with the garlic in a large frying pan over moderate heat. Reduce the clam liquid over high heat until full of flavour and then add it to the frying pan, pouring it slowly through a fine sieve and leaving behind any sand. Cook for 1 minute over high heat and then add the lemon rind, a pinch of salt, chilli, oregano and parsley. Mix well.

When the pasta is ready, drain and turn it into the frying pan. Add the shelled clams and stir-fry for no longer than 1 minute, using two forks to separate all the strands. Divide the spaghetti among four warmed plates and put some clams in their shells on top of each mound of spaghetti.

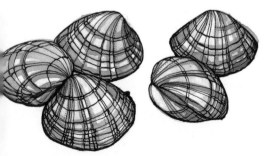

Fregola con le vongole

{ Fregola with clams }

Serves 4

1kg/2lb 4oz fresh live clams
in their shells

2 tbsp olive oil

1 banana shallot,
finely chopped

2 garlic cloves,
finely chopped

½ tsp crushed dried chillies

1 tbsp tomato purée (paste)

4 tbsp dry red vermouth

750ml/1¼ pints/3 cups fish
stock

200g/7oz fregola

3 tbsp chopped flat-leaf
parsley

olio santo (page 64), to serve
(optional)

Fregola is a very old type of pasta from southern Sardinia. The durum wheat semolina is mixed with water, salt and a little saffron in a large wooden bowl. When the dough is well kneaded together, it is rolled out until lots of small grains of different size are formed. The grains are then dried in the sun; they are always cooked in some sort of stock. Fregola is a pasta so important in Sardinian life that the ability to make good fregola – and it is not easy – was considered one of the virtues a girl must have to find a husband, just as the making of perfect tagliatelle was in Emilia-Romagna.

Dried fregola is now available in most delicatessens. I like very much the recipe in *Nigellissima*, Nigella Lawson's excellent and clever book on Italian food, so much so that I asked her if I could include it here. The only difference is that I use palourdes and no other clams, and fish stock rather than chicken. And I put my bottle of olio santo on the table for the final blessing.

Soak the clams in a sink full of cold water and go through them carefully; throw away any that remain open after you tap them on a hard surface, and any with a cracked shell.

While the clams are soaking, heat the oil in a large sauté pan. Throw in the shallot and cook for a minute, then add the garlic and chilli and sauté gently until the garlic begins to turn golden. Stir in the tomato purée, splash with the vermouth and add the stock. When the stock comes to the boil, mix in the fregola and simmer for 10–12 minutes. The fregola should be completely covered by the stock; if not, add some boiling water.

When the fregola are nearly cooked, gently lift the clams out of the water, leaving all the sand at the bottom of the sink, and put them into the pan. Put the lid on the pan and cook over high heat for 3 minutes. The clams should all be opened by now, but have a look through them and throw away any that remain closed. Mix in the parsley and ladle into four bowls. If you have it, put the bottle of olio santo on the table.

Spaghetti e calamari al pesto

{ Spaghetti with squid and pesto }

Serves 4

800g/1lb 12oz squid, cleaned
   and peeled

375g/13oz spaghetti

2 tbsp extra virgin olive oil

2 garlic cloves, crushed

Pesto

40g/1½oz fresh basil leaves

30g/1oz/3 tbsp pine nuts

2 garlic cloves

salt and freshly ground black
   pepper

6 tbsp extra virgin olive oil

This is a modern and very successful marriage of two Italian favourites, squid and pesto. The pesto here is made without cheese. Ask your fishmonger to clean the squid for you, reserving the tentacles, or follow the instructions for preparing squid on page 114.

First make the pesto following the method on page 138. Put it into a large serving bowl and keep warm in a very low oven (120°F/250°C/gas mark ½).

Cut the squid body sacs and flaps into small squares of about 2cm/¾ inch and cut the tentacles into short curly pieces.

Drop the spaghetti into a pan of boiling salted water.

Meanwhile, heat the oil with the garlic in a frying pan. When the garlic begins to turn golden, scoop it out and discard it. Slide the pieces of squid into the pan and stir-fry for 1–2 minutes, until they become opaque and milky-looking. Take the pan off the heat while you see to the pasta, which by now is nearly cooked.

When the pasta is ready, drain – do not overdrain – and transfer it immediately to the pesto bowl; mix well. Spoon the squid and all their delicious juices over the top and serve at once.

Kedgeree di orzo

{ Orzo kedgeree }

Serves 4

350g/12oz undyed smoked
 haddock

2 eggs

3 tbsp olive oil

2 onions, finely sliced

salt and freshly ground black
 pepper

1 tsp cayenne pepper

½ tsp ground turmeric

300g/10½oz orzo

50g/1¾oz/4 tbsp unsalted
 butter, cut into small pieces

125ml/4fl oz/½ cup double
 (heavy) cream

lemon juice

a bunch of flat-leaf parsley,
 chopped

One day I was all prepared to make a kedgeree, only to find out that I had no basmati rice. I thought of making the delicious risotto kedgeree from Nigella Lawson's *Feast* and then I decided to go one step further and make a pasta kedgeree. It worked and is very good. Any smallish pasta shapes, such as orzo, would do. Here is what I do.

Fill your pasta pot with water, without adding any salt, and put in the haddock. Bring to the boil, boil for 3 minutes and then turn off the heat. Lift the fish out of the water using a fish slice and, as soon as it is cool enough to handle, remove the skin and all the bones and flake it, but not too finely. Set aside. Reserve the fish cooking water.

Cook the eggs in boiling water for 8 minutes. Plunge them into cold water and then shell and chop them finely. Set aside.

Heat the oil in a large frying pan and, when hot, throw in the onions and season with a pinch of salt. Sauté for 20–25 minutes, until very soft, adding a little of the fish cooking water so that they cook gently without browning. Add the flaked fish, mix well and season with the cayenne and turmeric. Cook gently for 2 minutes, stirring frequently and adding a little more of the fish water whenever necessary. Taste and adjust the seasoning with salt and some pepper.

While the kedgeree is cooking, put the fish cooking water back on the heat. Add some salt and, when the water is boiling, add the orzo and cook until al dente.

When the pasta is ready, drain, reserving a cupful of the water, and turn the pasta into the pan with the fish. Add the butter and the chopped eggs and cook, stirring, for 2 minutes, adding a little of the pasta water to loosen the sauce. Pour in the cream, mix well and season with plenty of pepper and a squeeze or two of lemon juice. Scatter the parsley over the dish and serve at once.

Linguine al sugo di granchio

{ Linguine with crab sauce }

Serves 4

1 large crab

1 onion

1 celery stalk

1 bay leaf

salt

350g/12oz linguine

100ml/3½fl oz/scant ½ cup
  extra virgin olive oil

1 garlic clove, finely chopped

½–1 tsp crushed dried
  chillies, to taste

4 tbsp dry vermouth

about 2 dozen fresh basil
  leaves, coarsely chopped

olio santo (page 64)

I had this dish in Venice, where the sauce was made with the delicious *granceola* – the local spider crab. Away from the Mediterranean you can use regular crab, which has a similar, although slightly coarser, flavour. I have also made this sauce with ready-prepared crabmeat (an easier job) and used some fish stock to add at the end

Open the shell and crack the claws of the crab, scoop out all the white and dark meat and set it aside. Put the shell, the claws and all the discarded bits in a saucepan together with the onion, celery and bay leaf. Cover with 300ml/ 10fl oz/1¼ cups of cold water, bring to the boil and boil, uncovered, for 20 minutes. Strain and measure the liquid. You need no more than 200ml/ 7fl oz/generous ¾ cup. If you have more, put the liquid back on the heat and reduce over high heat. Set aside.

Drop the linguine into a pan of boiling salted water.

While the pasta is cooking, heat the oil in a frying pan, add the garlic and chilli and fry until the garlic begins to turn golden, about 1 minute. Throw in the crabmeat and mix, then add the vermouth and let it bubble away over high heat for a minute or two, while you shred the crabmeat with a fork. Pour in about 100ml/3½fl oz/scant ½ cup of the crab stock and cook for no more than 5 minutes. Season with salt to taste. If the pasta is not ready, remove the pan from the heat.

Drain the pasta and turn it into the pan with the crab. Add a little more crab stock if the pasta seems too dry. Put the pan back on the heat for a minute or two, using two forks to mix the whole thing thoroughly. Sprinkle the basil leaves over the dish before you serve it. Put the bottle of olio santo on the table for everybody to give it a final blessing of a few drops.

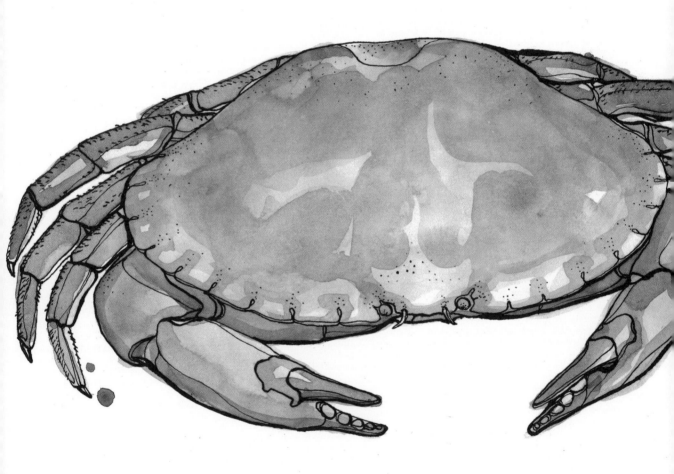

Bigoli in salsa

{ Bigoli in a sardine sauce }

Serves 6

100ml/3½fl oz/scant ½ cup
  extra virgin olive oil

250g/9oz red onions, very
  finely sliced

salt and freshly ground
  black pepper

150g/5½oz sardines
  preserved in olive oil

450g/1lb bigoli or
  wholewheat spaghetti

Bigoli, from Veneto, are the only pasta traditionally made with wholewheat flour, a little butter and duck eggs. They are like thick spaghetti and are dressed with a sardine or anchovy sauce (see below), a chicken liver sauce (*bigoli coi rovinazzi*) or a sauce of duck giblets and onion (*bigoli all'anara*). For this recipe, buy a good (expensive) brand of sardines. You can substitute anchovies for the sardines, in which case 70g/2½oz of anchovies, preferably preserved in salt, are enough.

Heat half the oil in a sauté pan and gently cook the onions with a pinch or two of salt, stirring frequently. When they begin to turn golden, add 3–4 tablespoons of hot water, cover the pan and cook for a further 20 minutes. Keep checking, and add a little more hot water whenever the sauce gets too dry.

Throw in the sardines and cook for about 2 minutes, while you mash them with a fork. Season with plenty of pepper.

While the sauce is cooking, cook the pasta in boiling salted water. When the pasta is ready, drain and turn it into a warmed bowl. Spoon over the sauce, pour over the remaining oil and mix very well. Serve at once with no Parmesan, the addition of which would be, for Italians, a sacrilege.

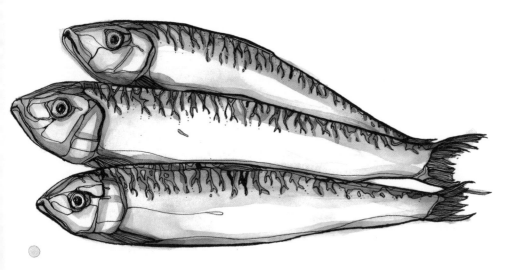

Spaghetti con uova di aringhe

{ Spaghetti with soft roes }

Serves 4

6 tbsp extra virgin olive oil

250g/9oz fresh tomatoes, peeled, seeded and chopped, or chopped canned plum tomatoes, drained

½–1 tsp crushed dried chillies, to taste

2 garlic cloves, finely chopped

350g/12oz spaghetti

250g/9oz soft roes

salt and freshly ground black pepper

4 tbsp chopped flat-leaf parsley

The soft roes, which are actually the milt of the male fish, are more delicate than the hard roes from the female.

Heat half the oil in a heavy-bottomed frying pan over high heat. Add the tomatoes, chilli and garlic and cook for 8–10 minutes.

Drop the spaghetti into a pan of boiling salted water.

Turn down the heat under the tomato sauce, add the roes and cook gently for about 4–5 minutes, breaking up the roes with a wooden spoon. Season with salt and pepper to taste. Just before serving, stir in the parsley.

When the pasta is ready, drain and return it to the pan in which it was cooked. Toss first with the remaining oil, and then with the roe sauce. Serve at once. No cheese is needed.

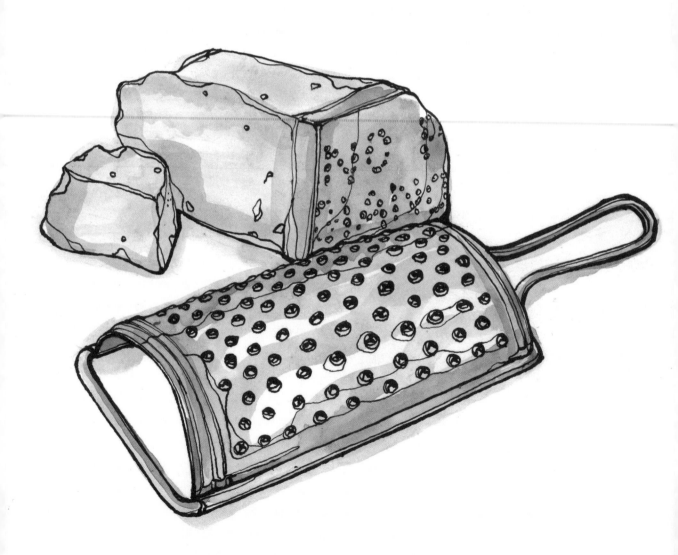

Dairy

Many cheeses are a good dressing for most shapes
of pasta. Cream adds a voluptuous delicacy to
many sauces, but it must be used
with restraint.

Tagliatelle all'inglese

{ *Tagliatelle with butter and cheese* }

Serves 4

homemade tagliatelle
(pages 58–61) made with
200g/7oz Italian 00 flour
and 2 eggs, or 300g/10½oz
dried egg tagliatelle

125g/4½oz/½ cup unsalted
butter, cut into small pieces

salt and freshly ground
black pepper

100g/3½oz Parmesan cheese,
grated

In northern Italy, food dressed only with butter is called 'all'inglese' – in the English style. However, a lot of Parmesan is also added for good measure, and it is indeed a very good measure. Try to get the best unsalted butter; some Italian ones are now available in many supermarkets and delicatessens. Expensive, I agree, but it makes all the difference.

Preheat the oven to 120°C/250°F/gas mark ½. Put the small pieces of butter into a serving bowl. Put the bowl into the oven, just to get warm.

Cook the tagliatelle in boiling salted water. Drain, reserving a cupful of the water, and transfer to the warmed bowl. Mix well and add a generous grinding of black pepper, half the Parmesan and a little of the reserved water, until the tagliatelle are all slippery. Serve at once, with the remaining cheese on the side.

Variations

• *Melt 1 teaspoon of Marmite in 1 tablespoon of the water in which the pasta was boiled and add to the pasta as you mix it with the butter and cheese. (I created this variation for my Marmite-loving son Guy.)*

• *In a small saucepan, very gently sauté the butter together with a few torn fresh sage leaves and 1 clove of crushed garlic until just golden, taking care not to burn the sauce. Pour over the drained pasta, sprinkle with 2 or 3 tablespoons of the Parmesan and mix well. Serve with the remaining Parmesan on the side.*

• *Fettuccine all'Alfredo*
This famous dish is the Roman answer to the classic northern Italian dish, tagliatelle all'inglese. The restaurateur Alfredo Di Lelio adapted it and served it in his restaurant in Rome to Mary Pickford and Douglas Fairbanks in 1914. They loved it. Alfredo II, his son, prepared the dish for Richard Burton and Elizabeth Taylor when they were in Rome filming Cleopatra – he served it with a golden spoon and a golden fork. And so fettuccine all'Alfredo became the signature dish of the restaurant, now run by the third generation of Alfredos. The difference between the humble Milanese tagliatelle all'inglese and this dish is in the amount of butter, nearly double in the Alfredo version, plus a glug of double (heavy) cream added for good measure, which I find really too rich. And, of course, the use of the Roman fettuccine, which are slightly thicker, but cut slightly narrower than the northern Italian tagliatelle.

Spaghetti con salsa rinascimentale

{ Spaghetti with almonds, ricotta and sweet spices }

Serves 4

100g/3½oz/¾ cup blanched
  almonds

30g/1oz/3½ tbsp almonds in
  their skins

50g/1¾oz/4 tbsp unsalted
  butter, cut into small pieces

150g/5½oz/generous ½ cup
  ricotta

30g/1oz Parmesan cheese,
  grated, plus extra to serve

1 tsp caster (superfine) sugar

2 tsp ground cinnamon

1 tsp freshly grated nutmeg

½ tsp ground cloves

125ml/4fl oz/½ cup double
  (heavy) cream

1 tbsp olive oil

2 tsp lemon juice

salt and freshly ground
  black pepper

350g/12oz spaghetti

a dozen sage leaves, torn

I love this sauce with the sweet and savoury flavour of the past. It is a recipe by Christoforo di Messisbugo, steward to the Duke d'Este of Ferrara in the sixteenth century. The Estes were great patrons of the arts and lovers of good living. As recorded in Messisbugo's book, their lavish banquets were unrivalled in the whole of Europe for their sumptuousness. This pasta sauce is, however, very simple to make and it has an unusual and subtle taste.
I add some almonds in their skins for additional flavour.

Preheat the oven to 180°C/350°F/gas mark 4.

Spread all the almonds on a baking sheet, place in the oven and bake for about 10–15 minutes, shaking the baking sheet once or twice during the time. Keep an eye on the almonds; they should just become golden, not burn – you can smell their aroma when they are ready. Turn off the oven, put the butter into a serving bowl and put the bowl into the oven to warm.

Blitz the almonds in a food processor to a grainy mixture. Tip them into the warmed bowl with the butter and add the ricotta, Parmesan, sugar, cinnamon, nutmeg, cloves, cream, oil, 1 teaspoon of the lemon juice, salt to taste and plenty of pepper. Mix thoroughly – use a fork rather than a spoon – and then taste and check the seasoning, adding more lemon juice if necessary.

Cook the spaghetti in boiling salted water. Drain, reserving a cupful of the water, and turn it into the serving bowl. Mix very thoroughly, using two forks, until all the strands are well coated, adding a couple of tablespoons of the pasta water to loosen the sauce. Sprinkle the sage leaves over the top and serve at once, with a bowl of grated Parmesan on the side.

Reginette al Gorgonzola

{ Reginette with Gorgonzola and ricotta }

Serves 4

350g/12oz reginette

½ garlic clove, chopped

1 small celery stalk, chopped

200g/7oz Gorgonzola cheese

100g/3½oz/scant ½ cup
ricotta

125ml/4fl oz/½ cup double
(heavy) cream

salt and freshly ground
black pepper

50g/1¾oz/4 tbsp unsalted
butter, cut into small pieces

freshly grated Parmesan
cheese, to serve

The pasta I use here is reginette, which means 'little queens'. They are also called mafalde and were created in 1902 for the birth of Princess Mafalda, daughter of the King of Italy. They are broad ribbons with ruffled edges and they go very well with any cheese or mushroom sauce. This simple sauce is ready in less time than it takes the pasta to cook.

Cook the pasta in boiling salted water.

While the pasta is cooking, put the garlic and celery in a food processor and blitz for a few seconds. Add the Gorgonzola, ricotta and cream and blitz again until thoroughly blended. Season with plenty of pepper and a pinch or two of salt – not much, because the Gorgonzola can be quite salty, so taste before you add it.

When the pasta is ready, drain, reserving a little of the water. Turn the pasta into a warmed serving bowl, toss with the butter, and then add the sauce and some of the pasta water to loosen the sauce, if necessary. Mix thoroughly and serve at once, with a bowl of grated Parmesan on the side.

Variation
Instead of garlic and pepper use 1 tablespoon of chopped spring onion (scallion) and 1 heaped teaspoon of paprika.

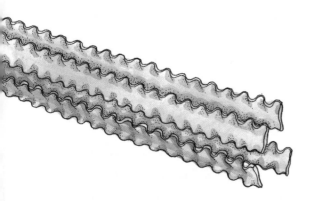

Conchigliette con salsa di Gorgonzola, pistacchi e cognac

{ Small shells with Gorgonzola, pistachios and brandy }

Serves 4

75g/2¾oz/generous ½ cup
  shelled pistachio nuts

350g/12oz small pasta shells

50g/1¾oz/4 tbsp unsalted
  butter, cut into small pieces

200g/7oz Gorgonzola cheese,
  cut into small cubes

150ml/5fl oz/⅔ cup double
  (heavy) cream

2 tbsp brandy

salt and freshly ground
  black pepper

This sauce is made up of some unlikely ingredients, but the result is one of the best sauces ever. The pistachios needed here are the fresh nuts in their green skin.

Put the pistachio nuts in a small bowl and cover with boiling water. Let stand for 2–3 minutes, and then drain and dry them with kitchen paper. Remove as much as you can of the skin and then pound the nuts with a mortar and pestle or blitz them in a food processor.

Cook the pasta in boiling salted water.

In a small, heavy-bottomed saucepan, melt the butter with the cheese, stirring constantly, without letting the mixture come to the boil. As soon as they have melted, add the cream and cook very gently for 5 minutes, stirring constantly. Remove from the heat and add the pistachios and brandy. Taste and adjust the seasoning.

When the pasta is ready, drain, reserving a cupful of the water. Turn the pasta into a warmed bowl or back into the pot in which it has cooked and mix in the sauce. If necessary, add 2–3 tablespoons of the pasta water to loosen the sauce. Serve at once.

Frittata di pasta

{ Pasta frittata }

Serves 4

about 400g/14oz leftover
   pasta, or 200g/7oz
   raw pasta

4 eggs

50g/1¾oz Parmesan cheese,
   grated

2 tbsp chopped fresh parsley

salt and freshly ground
   black pepper

4 tbsp olive oil

30g/1oz/2 tbsp unsalted
   butter, cut into small pieces

This is the best way to finish up any leftover pasta dressed with a vegetable or cheese sauce. Depending on how much pasta you have left, adjust the quantities of all other ingredients accordingly. Of course, you can also make the frittata from scratch, by cooking the pasta and then leaving it to cool.

If you are using raw pasta, cook it in boiling salted water, drain, toss with 1 tablespoon of olive oil, and leave to cool. If you are using leftover long pasta such as spaghetti, cut the strands into short lengths of 10–12 cm/about 4 inches.

Put the cooked pasta into a large bowl and add the eggs, cheese, parsley, salt and pepper. Mix very thoroughly.

Preheat the grill. Heat the oil in a 25 cm/10 inch non-stick frying pan. When hot, add the pasta mixture and spread it evenly all over the bottom of the pan. Press it down gently and cook over low heat for about 15 minutes, occasionally using a wooden spatula to lift the side and prevent it from sticking. Dot little pieces of the butter over the top and place the pan under the hot grill for about 1 minute, or until the top is cooked and just golden. Cut into wedges and serve.

Tagliatelle in salsa di mascarpone, pomodoro e basilico

{ Tagliatelle with mascarpone, tomato and basil }

Serves 4

homemade tagliatelle
  (pages 58–61) made with
  200g/7oz Italian 00 flour
  and 2 eggs, or 300g/10½oz
  dried egg tagliatelle

50g/1¾oz/4 tbsp unsalted
  butter

1 garlic clove, crushed

500g/1lb 2oz ripe tomatoes,
  peeled and seeded

2 tbsp passata (strained
  tomatoes)

125g/4½oz/½ cup
  mascarpone cheese

½ tsp crushed dried chillies

a dozen fresh basil leaves,
  torn into pieces

freshly grated Parmesan
  cheese, to serve

A very easy sauce with a delicate, yet distinctive flavour.

If you are making the pasta at home, follow the instructions on pages 58–61.

Preheat the oven to 120°C/250°F/gas mark ½.

In a saucepan, heat the butter with the garlic, add the tomatoes and cook for 3–4 minutes over high heat. Mix in the passata and continue cooking for a couple of minutes. Spoon in the mascarpone, season with the chilli, salt and pepper and bring the sauce to the boil. Simmer for a minute or two, stirring constantly, and then transfer the sauce to a serving bowl. Put the bowl in the oven while you cook the pasta.

When the tagliatelle are ready, reserve a cupful of the water and drain, but do not overdrain. Transfer the tagliatelle to the bowl with the sauce and mix well, adding a little of the pasta water to loosen the sauce. Scatter with the basil leaves and serve at once, with a bowl of grated Parmesan on the side.

Vegetables

Pasta of any shape and vegetables of any variety are a natural combination. The following recipes are all *cucina povera* recipes, *povera* meaning 'homely' but certainly not poor. In fact these are some of the best pasta sauces I know.

Vermicelli al sugo del settecento

{ Vermicelli with sweet-and-sour tomato sauce }

Serves 4

plain tomato sauce
 (see page 72) made with
 1kg/2lb 4oz tomatoes

125ml/4fl oz/½ cup extra
 virgin olive oil

2 garlic cloves, lightly
 crushed

½ tsp crushed dried chillies

½ tsp ground cinnamon, or
 more, according to taste

1 tsp sugar

350g/12oz vermicelli or
 spaghettini (thin spaghetti)

100g/3½oz Parmesan cheese,
 grated

This is an eighteenth-century recipe from the book *Il Cuoco Galante* by Vincenzo Corrado. Corrado gathered a great number of recipes, which I have always found very inspirational. This recipe is one of the first to combine pasta with the newly popular tomato.

At least 1 hour before you want to eat, put the tomato sauce into a large serving bowl and add the oil, garlic, spices and sugar. This will allow time for the flavours to blend.

Preheat the oven to 120°C/250°F/gas mark ½. Put the bowl with the sauce into the oven to warm through.

Cook the spaghetti in boiling salted water.

Remove the garlic cloves from the sauce and, when the pasta is ready, drain and turn it into the bowl with the sauce. Sprinkle with half the grated Parmesan and mix thoroughly. Serve at once, with the remaining Parmesan in a bowl on the side.

Farfalle con panna e cipolla

{ Farfalle with cream and onion }

Serves 4

350g/12oz farfalle

30g/1oz/2 tbsp unsalted butter

2 tbsp olive oil

4 tbsp grated red onion

salt and freshly ground black pepper

125ml/4fl oz/½ cup double (heavy) cream

50g/1¾oz Parmesan cheese, grated, plus extra to serve

2 tbsp chopped flat-leaf parsley

A very quick and delicious sauce that takes no longer to cook than the pasta.

Cook the farfalle in boiling salted water.

While the pasta is cooking, heat the butter and oil in a large frying pan. When the foam begins to subside, throw in the onion and a pinch or two of salt and cook gently for 7–8 minutes, stirring very frequently and adding 2 or 3 tablespoons of the pasta water as it cooks. The onion should not become golden, just soft.

When the farfalle are ready, drain and transfer them to the frying pan. Add the cream, cheese and lots of pepper and stir-fry for a couple of minutes. Sprinkle with the parsley and serve at once, with a bowl of grated Parmesan on the side.

Spaghetti olio, aglio e peperoncino

{ Spaghetti with oil, garlic and chilli }

Serves 4

350g/12oz spaghetti or linguine

salt

6 tbsp extra virgin olive oil

3–4 garlic cloves, finely chopped

½–1 tsp crushed dried chillies, to taste

3 tbsp chopped flat-leaf parsley

This is the most flavourful quick sauce I know. Every time I eat it I think it is the best way to dress spaghetti.

Cook the spaghetti in boiling salted water.

While the pasta is cooking, heat the oil in a large frying pan. Add the garlic, chilli and half the parsley and sauté for 2–3 minutes.

When the pasta is ready, drain, but do not overdrain, and tip it into the frying pan. Stir-fry for 2 minutes, using two forks to lift the strands high so that they all get coated with oil. Sprinkle with the remaining parsley and serve at once. No cheese is served with this sauce.

Trenette al pesto genovese

{ Trenette with pesto }

Serves 4

1 heaped tablespoon sea salt

200g/7oz new potatoes,
   peeled and cut into
   small cubes

200g/7oz green beans,
   topped and tailed and cut
   into 2cm/¾ inch length

300g/10½oz trenette or trofie

freshly grated pecorino or
   Parmesan cheese, to serve
   (optional)

Pesto

about 50g/1¾oz fresh basil
   leaves (the leaves from a
   large bunch of basil)

2 tbsp pine nuts

2 garlic cloves

½ tsp sea salt crystals

freshly ground black pepper

4 tbsp freshly grated
   Parmesan cheese

2 tbsp freshly grated
   pecorino cheese

100ml/3½fl oz/scant ½ cup
   olive oil

This is the recipe for the traditional pesto alla Genovese, in which the pasta is cooked with potato and green beans. If you prefer, you can leave them out. Trenette and trofie are the best-known pasta shapes of Liguria. Trenette are long, thin strands, similar to linguine, traditionally associated with this dish.

Pesto freezes perfectly, so it can be made in quantity while basil is in season and brought out during the rest of the year. When making the sauce for the freezer, omit the cheese, and fold it in just before serving.

First, make the pesto. In a large mortar, preferably marble, pound the basil leaves, pine nuts, garlic, salt and pepper together until they form a thick paste. Using a wooden spoon, fold in the cheeses, and then, very slowly, the oil. Let stand for at least 1 hour.

Spoon the pesto into a large serving bowl and keep warm in a very low oven (120°F/250°C/gas mark ½).

Put a large saucepan of water on the heat and, when boiling add the salt and the potatoes. Boil for 5 minutes and then throw in the beans. Boil for 4 minutes, add the pasta and cook until al dente.

When the pasta is ready, drain, reserving a cupful of the water. Turn the pasta into the bowl with the pesto and mix well, adding 2–3 or more tablespoons of the reserved water to loosen the sauce. Serve at once, with more grated cheese if you wish.

_____

Blender pesto
Pesto can be made very quickly in a food processor or a blender. It is not as good, maybe, but the difference in flavour is quite minimal, while the difference in time is quite substantial.

Use the same ingredients as above. Combine the basil, pine nuts, garlic, salt and pepper in a food processor or blender and whizz while you add the oil through the funnel until the mixture forms a paste. Transfer the pesto to a bowl and fold in the grated cheeses.

A lighter pesto

50–60g/1¾–2¼oz fresh
  basil leaves

1 tbsp roughly chopped
  parsley

50g/1¾oz/6 tbsp pine nuts

1 garlic clove, chopped

1 tsp salt

freshly ground black pepper

75ml/2½fl oz/5 tbsp extra
  virgin olive oil

30g/1oz/2 tbsp unsalted
  butter

30g/1oz Parmesan cheese,
  freshly grated

30g/1oz pecorino cheese,
  freshly grated

1 tbsp Greek-style yogurt

**The following recipe is a more sophisticated version, and the result is a more
delicate sauce.**

Combine the basil, parsley, pine nuts, garlic, salt and pepper in a food processor
or blender and whizz while you add the oil through the funnel until you have a
paste. Spoon the pesto into a serving bowl, add the butter, cheeses and yogurt
and place the bowl in a very low oven (120°F/250°C/gas mark ½).

Cook the pasta as usual and when al dente, drain, reserving a cupful of the
water. Turn the pasta into the bowl, add a few tablespoons of the reserved water
and mix thoroughly.

Fusilli al pesto rosso

{ Fusilli with red pesto }

Serves 5–6

2 red peppers

50g/1¾oz/6 tbsp pine nuts

50g/1¾oz/⅓ cup almonds in
their skins

2 garlic cloves

½ tsp crushed dried chillies

salt and freshly ground
black pepper

6 tbsp extra virgin olive oil

1 tbsp lemon juice

500g/1lb 2oz fusilli or
linguine

a dozen black olives, pitted

1 tbsp olio santo (page 64)

This is a Sicilian pesto made with peppers, chilli and almonds.

Put the peppers on a direct flame or under the grill and grill until the outer skin is black and blistered. Turn the peppers around and continue roasting them until the skin is charred all over. Quarter and peel the peppers carefully, discarding the seeds and the ribs.

Preheat the oven to 120°C/250°F/gas mark ½.

Dry-fry the pine nuts and almonds in a cast-iron or heavy-bottomed pan. As soon as the nuts begin to colour, tip them into a food processor.

Add the peppers, garlic, chilli, salt and pepper and blitz while you add the oil through the funnel. When the mixture is of a grainy consistency, tip it into a serving bowl. Mix in the lemon juice, taste and adjust the seasoning. Put the bowl in the oven.

Cook the pasta in boiling salted water. Drain when it is just al dente, reserving a cupful of the water. Tip the pasta into the sauce and mix thoroughly. Add 3 or 4 tablespoons of the reserved water to loosen the sauce. Scatter with the olives, pour over the olio santo and serve at once.

Tonnarelli al pesto di rucola

{ Tonnarelli with rocket pesto }

Serves 4

50g/1¾oz/6 tbsp pine nuts

100g/3½oz rocket (arugula)

1 garlic clove

salt and freshly ground
black pepper

125ml/4fl oz/½ cup extra
virgin olive oil

50g/1¾oz pecorino cheese,
grated

350g/12oz tonnarelli
or spaghetti

50g/1¾oz Parmesan cheese,
grated

Pesto sauces of different ingredients are very quick to make and very good to eat. This is a relatively new pesto sauce, which can be made all the year round now that rocket is always available. What all these pesto sauces need is the best olive oil, and, of course, fresh nuts. That's all.

Preheat the oven to 120°C/250°F/gas mark ½.

Dry-fry the pine nuts in a cast-iron or heavy-bottomed pan for a few minutes, until they release their aroma, being careful not to let them burn. When they are golden, tip them into a food processor or blender.

Add the rocket, garlic, some pepper and 4 tablespoons of the oil and blitz while you add the remaining oil through the funnel until everything is well blended. Taste and adjust the seasoning, then spoon the pesto into a serving bowl. Mix in the pecorino and put the bowl in the oven.

Cook the pasta in boiling salted water. Drain when it is just al dente, reserving a cupful of the water. Tip the pasta into the sauce and mix thoroughly, adding a little of the reserved water to loosen the sauce. Serve at once with the grated Parmesan on the side.

Spaghettini al pesto di pistacchi

{ Spaghettini with pistachio pesto }

Serves 4

150g/5½oz/generous 1 cup
shelled pistachio nuts

30g/1oz/3½ tbsp pine nuts

1 garlic clove

a grating of nutmeg

125ml/4fl oz/½ cup extra
virgin olive oil

salt and freshly ground
black pepper

350g/12oz spaghettini or
spaghetti

30g/1oz Parmesan cheese,
grated, plus extra to serve

For this pesto you need the fresh pistachio nuts in their skins, but not in their shells.

Preheat the oven to 120°C/250°F/gas mark ½.

Put the pistachio nuts in a bowl and cover them with boiling water. Set aside. Dry-fry the pine nuts in a cast-iron or heavy-bottomed pan for a few minutes, until golden, being careful not to let them burn. Tip them into a food processor or blender.

Now drain the pistachio nuts and remove as much as you can of the bluish-green skin. Dry them on kitchen paper and put them in the food processor with the pine nuts. Add the garlic and nutmeg and blitz while you add the oil through the funnel. Taste and adjust the seasoning, then spoon the pesto into a serving bowl and put the bowl in the oven.

Cook the spaghetti in boiling salted water. Drain when it is just al dente, reserving a cupful of the water. Tip the spaghetti into the bowl, add the pesto and mix well, adding a little of the reserved water to loosen the sauce. Serve at once with a bowl of grated Parmesan.

Pesto alla trapanese

{ Pesto with almonds and cherry tomatoes }

Serves 4

35g/1¼oz/4 tbsp blanched
  almonds

15g/½oz/2 tbsp almonds in
  their skins

about 7–8 ripe cherry
  tomatoes, peeled, seeded
  and chopped

2 garlic cloves

about 24 fresh basil leaves

salt and freshly ground
  black pepper

125ml/4fl oz/½ cup extra
  virgin olive oil

50g/1¾oz ricotta salata,
  grated

350g/12oz bucatini
  or spaghetti

freshly grated Parmesan
  cheese, to serve (optional)

Like the basil pesto made in Liguria, this pesto sauce has been made for centuries in Trapani, a town on the western coast of Sicily. Originally it was made without the tomatoes, but in the eighteenth century, when tomatoes became a staple of local food, they were added to the pesto.

I always leave some of the almonds in their skins because the skin adds flavour to the dish. Like all other uncooked sauces, this pesto needs the best ingredients – and the result is fabulous. If you cannot find *ricotta salata* (dried salted ricotta, available from some Italian or online), use pecorino.

Preheat the oven to 120°C/250°F/gas mark ½.

Dry-fry the almonds in a cast-iron or heavy-bottomed pan for a few minutes, until they release their aroma, then tip them into a food processor. Blitz until they are reduced to the size of rice grains and then add the tomatoes, garlic, basil and salt and pepper to taste. Blitz again while you add half the oil through the funnel, until everything is blended. Spoon the pesto into a serving bowl, mix in the ricotta salata and put the bowl in the oven.

Cook the bucatini in boiling salted water. Drain when it is just al dente, reserving a cupful of the water. Tip the pasta into the bowl and mix thoroughly, adding a little of the pasta water to loosen the sauce. Serve at once, with a bowl of grated Parmesan if you like.

Pomodori ripieni di pasta

{ Tomatoes stuffed with pasta }

Serves 4 as an antipasto

2 large ripe tomatoes

salt

125g/4½oz ditalini or maccheroncini

50g/1¾oz rocket (arugula), preferably wild, torn into small pieces

5 tbsp extra virgin olive oil

1 tbsp lemon juice

2 garlic cloves, thinly sliced

½ tsp crushed dried chillies

2 salted anchovies, cleaned and rinsed, or 4 anchovy fillets, drained

This is a cheerful summer antipasto or an excellent lunch dish, in which case you must double the quantities. It needs small pasta shapes and good tomatoes.

Slice off the top of each tomato and discard. Scoop out and discard the seeds and pulp, sprinkle with salt and leave to drain, cut side down on kitchen paper, for about 1 hour.

While the tomatoes are draining, cook the pasta in boiling salted water. Drain when just al dente (pasta served cold must be slightly undercooked) and turn it into a bowl. Add the rocket, 2 tablespoons of the oil and the lemon juice. Mix well.

Heat the remaining oil in a large frying pan and add the garlic, chilli and anchovies. Cook for 1–2 minutes, stirring and squashing the anchovies against the pan. Add the pasta and rocket mixture to the pan and stir-fry for 1–2 minutes. Taste and adjust the seasoning.

Dry the inside of the tomatoes with kitchen paper and fill them with the pasta mixture. Serve at room temperature.

Maccheroncini alla purè di cannnellini

{ Maccheroncini with cannellini purée }

Serves 4

350g/12oz maccheroncini

1 x 400g/14oz can cannellini
  beans

1 garlic clove,
  roughly chopped

a generous handful of flat-leaf
  parsley, stalks removed

½–1 tsp crushed dried
  chillies, to taste

100ml/3½fl oz/scant ½ cup
  extra virgin olive oil

salt

a dozen basil leaves,
  torn into pieces

freshly grated pecorino
  cheese, to serve

I like to use a small shape pasta for this extremely easy and quick sauce. Frankly, I have no idea how it came into my repertoire. I am pretty sure I must first have had it in the 1970s, when we had a house in Chianti; anything with cannellini beans and chilli is Tuscan. Use a strong peppery olive oil. Maccheroncini are narrower and shorter than macaroni; if you can't find them, you could use ditalini or gnocchetti sardi.

Preheat the oven to 120°C/250°F/gas mark ½. Cook the pasta in boiling salted water.

While the pasta is cooking, drain the beans, reserving the liquid, and put them into a food processor. Add the garlic, parsley, chilli and half the olive oil. Blitz to a purée, adding 3–4 tablespoons of the reserved cannellini bean liquid. The sauce should have the consistency of double (heavy) cream. Taste and add salt. Spoon the sauce into a serving bowl and put the bowl in the oven to warm through.

When the pasta is ready, drain and transfer to the bowl. Pour over the remaining oil and mix everything together. Scatter with the torn basil leaves and serve at once with a bowl of grated pecorino.

Fusilli con le zucchini e i porri

{ Fusilli with courgette and leek sauce }

Serves 3–4

6 tbsp extra virgin olive oil

150g/5½oz leek (white part only), sliced in small rings or chopped

2 tbsp chopped flat-leaf parsley

500g/1lb 2oz courgettes (zucchini), cut into matchsticks

150ml/5fl oz/⅔ cup dry white wine

a grating of nutmeg

about 4–6 tbsp whole milk

375g/13oz fusilli, spirali or other short pasta

6 tbsp freshly grated Parmesan cheese, plus extra to serve

salt and freshly ground black pepper

a dozen fresh mint leaves

Courgettes are now available all the year round. Buy hard, shiny courgettes, neither too small – because baby courgettes have not yet fully developed their flavour – nor too big, because the big ones are full of seeds. The leeks should be thin, with fresh-looking green tops, which you don't need for this recipe but can keep for a soup. The combination of these two vegetables, both rather sweet, is sharpened here by a glass of wine. This is a well-balanced mixture of different yet harmonious flavours.

Heat half of the oil in a large frying pan with a lid. Throw in the leeks, sauté for a minute and then add the parsley and sauté for about 2 minutes. Add the courgettes and sauté for a minute or two, then splash with the wine and continue cooking for a few minutes, stirring frequently, until the wine has evaporated. Season with the nutmeg and add about 4 tablespoons of milk. Cover the pan, turn down the heat and cook until the courgettes are tender, which may take around 15 minutes. Check occasionally and add a little more milk whenever the sauce gets too dry.

While the sauce is cooking, cook the pasta in boiling salted water.

When the pasta is ready, drain, but do not overdrain, and transfer to the courgette pan. Mix in the remaining oil and the Parmesan and stir-fry for a minute or two. Taste and adjust the seasoning and scatter the mint over the top. Serve at once, and hand around a bowl of grated Parmesan.

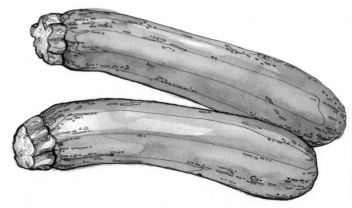

Trofie in salsa di noci

{ Trofie with walnut sauce }

Serves 4

100g/3½oz/scant 1 cup
  shelled walnuts

30g/1oz one-day-old
  crustless bread

3–4 tbsp whole milk

1 garlic clove

100ml/3½fl oz/scant ½ cup
  extra virgin olive oil

2 tbsp double (heavy) cream

50g/1¾oz Parmesan cheese,
  grated, plus extra to serve

salt and freshly ground
  black pepper

350g/12oz trofie

This sauce from Liguria is traditionally used with pansoti or corzetti, local pasta shapes made with a simple dough of flour and water. Pansoti are the Ligurian ravioli, filled with wild herbs, beet leaves, borage and ricotta. Corzetti come in two shapes: in one, the rolled-out dough is cut in the shape of a figure of eight; in the other, a far rarer shape, the dough is cut in the shape of large coins and each coin is stamped with a special wooden tool carved with a pattern. In the old days, aristocratic families had their own stamp with the coat of arms on it. Corzetti are rarely found on the market, but another Ligurian pasta shape, trofie, can be used; these are more widely available from supermarkets.

As for the walnuts, they should be fresh-looking with no dark spots and in large pieces, showing no sign of powder. Of all nuts, walnuts are the ones that most quickly turn rancid and they become unpleasantly acid when old.

Soak the walnuts in boiling water for about 15 minutes and then drain and remove as much of the skin as you can. Preheat the oven to 120°C/250°F/gas mark ½.

Break the bread into small pieces, put it in a bowl and pour over the milk. Leave it for a few minutes and then squeeze out the milk and put the bread in a food processor together with the walnuts and the garlic. Blitz while adding the oil through the funnel. Transfer the mixture to a serving bowl and mix in the cream and the Parmesan. Taste and season with salt and a little pepper. Place the bowl in the oven.

Cook the trofie in boiling salted water. Drain, reserving some of the water, and turn it into the bowl with the sauce. Add a little of the reserved pasta water to loosen the sauce, mix well and serve at once with a bowl of grated Parmesan.

Lumache coi funghi e piselli

{ Lumache with mushrooms and peas }

Serves 4

5 tbsp olive oil

1 garlic clove, very
  finely chopped

200g/7oz chestnut (cremini)
  mushrooms, finely sliced

4 tbsp dry white vermouth

salt and freshly ground
  black pepper

350g/12oz lumache or
  conchiglie

125g/4½oz/1 cup shelled
  peas or frozen petits pois

30g/1oz/2 tbsp unsalted
  butter, cut into small pieces

freshly grated Parmesan
  cheese, to serve

Lumache means 'snails', and this pasta shape looks like empty snail shells. Conchiglie would be just as good, but you could use any short chunky pasta.

Heat the oil in a large frying pan, add the garlic, and as soon as it begins to colour, throw in the mushrooms. Cook over lively heat for 5 minutes, stirring frequently. Splash with the vermouth and let it partly evaporate for a couple of minutes. Turn the heat down, season with salt and add 3 or 4 tablespoons of hot water. Cook for about 15 minutes.

While the mushrooms are cooking, cook the lumache in boiling salted water.

Add the peas to the mushrooms – if they are fresh, cook for 5 minutes; if frozen, 2 minutes is enough.

When the pasta is ready, drain, turn into the frying pan, add the butter and stir-fry for 2 minutes, turning everything over and over so that all the pasta shells are coated with the sauce. Taste and season with pepper and, if necessary, salt. Serve at once with a bowl of grated Parmesan.

Spaghettini con i porri

{ Thin spaghetti with leeks }

Serves 4

30g/1oz/2 tbsp unsalted
  butter

2 tbsp olive oil

1kg/2lb 4oz leeks (white
  part only), sliced into
  very thin rings and
  washed thoroughly

salt and freshly ground
  black pepper

1 tsp curry powder

125ml/4fl oz/½ cup
  vegetable or chicken stock

350g/12oz spaghettini
  (thin spaghetti)

4 tbsp double (heavy) cream

100g/3½oz Parmesan cheese,
  grated

I use ready-made curry powder for this sauce since it is not worth blending the spices from scratch for such a small amount. Keep the green parts of the leeks to make soup.

In a large frying pan, heat half the butter and the oil. Add the leeks, a little salt and the curry powder and sauté gently for 2 minutes. Now add half the stock and cook, covered, over very low heat for about 30 minutes, adding a little more stock whenever necessary, so that the leeks are always cooking in some liquid. At the end the leeks should have collapsed to a mushy consistency. Taste and adjust the seasoning.

Cook the pasta in boiling salted water. Drain, reserving a cupful of the water, and transfer the pasta to the frying pan, add the cream, the remaining butter, half the Parmesan and some of the pasta water. Using two forks, mix thoroughly over low heat for 2 minutes and then serve at once, with the remaining Parmesan on the side.

Reginette ai funghi, prezzemolo e mascarpone

{ Reginette with mushrooms, parsley and mascarpone sauce }

Serves 4

100ml/3½fl oz/scant ½ cup
  whole milk

30g/1oz dried porcini

4 tbsp olive oil

1 garlic clove, finely chopped

4 tbsp chopped flat-leaf
  parsley

200g/7oz chestnut (cremini)
  mushrooms, sliced

salt and freshly ground
  black pepper

350g/12oz reginette

4 heaped tbsp mascarpone
  cheese

freshly grated Parmesan
  cheese, to serve

This is a delicate sauce with a good balance of flavours. Reginette are pasta ribbons with ruffled edges, also known as mafalde; ricciarelle are very similar.

Heat the milk, pour it over the dried porcini and leave to soak for 15–20 minutes. Drain, reserving the milk, and chop the porcini.

Heat the oil in a large frying pan, add the garlic and half the parsley, and cook over low heat for 1 minute, stirring constantly. Add the fresh mushrooms and the porcini and sauté for 15 minutes, adding a few tablespoons of the reserved porcini milk. Season with salt and pepper.

While the mushrooms are cooking, cook the pasta in boiling salted water. Drain and turn it into the frying pan. Mix in the mascarpone and stir-fry for about 2 minutes, turning the reginette over and over to thoroughly coat them with the sauce. Sprinkle with the remaining parsley and serve at once, with a bowl of grated Parmesan on the side.

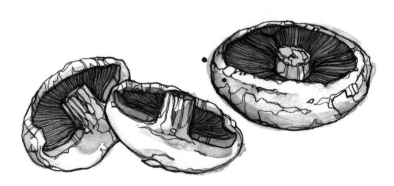

Garganelli alla boscaiola

{ Garganelli with porcini and tomatoes }

Serves 4

400g/14oz fresh porcini
(ceps)

6 tbsp extra virgin olive oil

1 small onion, finely chopped

1 small carrot, finely chopped

1 small celery stalk,
finely chopped

salt and freshly ground
black pepper

150ml/5fl oz/⅔ cup dry
white wine

250g/9oz canned
chopped tomatoes

3 tbsp chopped flat-leaf
parsley

300g/10½oz dried garganelli,
penne rigate or radiatori

freshly grated Parmesan
cheese, to serve

Garganelli are a pasta shape originally from Romagna. In that region garganelli are often still made at home with an egg and flour dough flavoured with grated Parmesan and/or grated nutmeg. The dough is rolled out thinly and cut into small squares, which are rolled around a smooth stick; the stick is then pressed over a comb-like wooden tool which creates grooves to hold the rich sauce with which they are traditionally dressed. Garganelli are also available dried.

This recipe is called *alla boscaiola* – 'in the woodland style' – in reference to the main ingredient: mushrooms. If you cannot find fresh porcini, use chestnut (cremini) mushrooms plus 30g/1oz of dried porcini, which must be soaked in hot water for 15–20 minutes before use.

To prepare the porcini, wipe them clean with kitchen paper. If large, cut off the stems and slice them vertically into slices about 3mm/⅛ inch thick. Do the same with the caps. If the porcini are small, slice cap and stem together, without separating them.

In a large sauté pan, heat 4 tablespoons of the oil, throw in the onion, sauté for 2–3 minutes and then add the carrot, celery and a good pinch of salt. Cook, stirring very frequently, for about 20 minutes, until the mixture is softened and golden.

Add the mushrooms and cook over moderately high heat for 5 minutes or so. Pour in the wine, let it bubble away for 2–3 minutes and then add the tomatoes and half the parsley. Cook over low heat for about 30 minutes, stirring frequently.

Meanwhile, cook the pasta in boiling salted water. Drain and turn it into the pan with the sauce. Add some pepper and salt to taste and the remaining oil and cook for 2 minutes, mixing thoroughly. Sprinkle with the remaining parsley and serve with plenty of grated Parmesan.

Insalata di orecchiette e broccoletti

{ Orecchiette and broccoli salad }

Serves 4

500g/1lb 2oz broccoli

350g/12oz orecchiette

6 tbsp extra virgin olive oil

3 tbsp pine nuts

1–2 garlic cloves, very
 finely chopped

2 salted anchovies, cleaned
 and rinsed, or 4 anchovy
 fillets, drained

½ tsp crushed dried chillies

salt

This dish is also very good hot. So I leave the choice to you. Orecchiette are one of the two traditional shapes used in Puglia, where this recipe originates, the other being cavatielli. Other good shapes for this sauce are fusilli or pennette.

Break the broccoli into very small florets. Cut the stalks into thin rounds – if they are thick, peel off the outer layers. Blanch the stalks and florets in boiling salted water for 2 minutes; drain and dry with kitchen paper.

Cook the orecchiette in boiling salted water until just al dente (pasta served cold must be slightly undercooked) and then drain. Put them in a serving bowl and dress with 1 tablespoon of the olive oil.

While the pasta is cooking, toast the pine nuts in a frying pan until just golden. Keep an eye on them because they burn very easily. Set aside.

In the same frying pan, heat 4 tablespoons of the oil, add the garlic, anchovies and chilli and fry for a minute or so, then add the broccoli. Sauté for 3 minutes, stirring frequently, and then taste and adjust the seasoning. Add to the pasta and mix well, but gently, using two forks, which are less likely to break the broccoli florets. Cover with clingfilm and leave until cold.

Before serving, pour over the remaining oil, which will give the dish a fresh look, and scatter the pine nuts over the top.

Spaghettini alla marinara

{ Spaghettini with fresh tomatoes }

Serves 4

750g/1lb 10oz ripe tomatoes, peeled

salt

350g/12oz spaghettini (thin spaghetti)

6 tbsp extra virgin olive oil

3 garlic cloves, crushed

½ tsp crushed dried chillies

a dozen fresh basil leaves, torn into pieces

You can make this sauce only with good fresh tomatoes. In Naples no cheese is served with this dish.

Cut each tomato into about six segments and discard the seeds. Lay them on a board, sprinkle with salt and leave for about 30 minutes. This salting brings out the flavour.

Cook the spaghettini in boiling salted water.

While the pasta is cooking, heat the oil in a large frying pan and when it is hot, but not smoking, add the garlic and chilli and cook for 1 minute. Add the tomatoes and cook for about 3 minutes, stirring all the time.

When the pasta is ready, drain and transfer it to the frying pan. Stir-fry for a couple of minutes, using two forks to separate the strands, and then sprinkle the basil over the top and serve at once.

Spaghettini alla moda di Umbertide

{ Thin spaghetti with tomatoes, bay leaves and cinnamon }

Serves 4

4 tbsp olive oil

1 large onion, finely chopped

750g/1lb 10oz fresh tomatoes, peeled and seeded, or canned chopped tomatoes

10 fresh bay leaves

½ tsp ground cinnamon

salt and freshly ground black pepper

350g/12oz spaghettini (thin spaghetti) or tagliolini

This old-fashioned recipe comes from the mountains around Perugia, the capital of Umbria, where bay trees grow wild. It has an unusual and delicious taste.

In a large frying pan, heat the oil and sauté the onion until translucent. Add the tomatoes (if you are using canned tomatoes, discard half of the juice), the bay leaves, cinnamon, salt and a fair amount of pepper. Cook, uncovered, for 15 minutes, stirring every now and then.

Cook the pasta in boiling salted water. Drain it, reserving a little of the water, then transfer it to the frying pan and stir-fry for a minute or two, adding a little of the reserved water to loosen the sauce. No cheese is served with this sauce.

Spaghetti alla puttanesca

{ Spaghetti with anchovy fillets and olives }

Serves 4

350g/12oz spaghetti

3–4 tbsp extra virgin olive oil

8 anchovy fillets, drained
and chopped, or 4 salted
anchovies, cleaned, rinsed
and chopped

2 garlic cloves, finely sliced

1 small fresh chilli, seeds and
ribs removed, sliced

500g/1lb 2oz fresh tomatoes,
peeled, seeded and cut into
thin strips

125g/4½oz/¾ cup black
olives, pitted and sliced

1 tbsp capers

salt

2 tbsp chopped flat-leaf
parsley

2 tbsp olio santo (page 64)

**This now-famous recipe from Rome has its origins in the poor district of
Trastevere, the traditional haunt of Roman prostitutes. Its name (a *puttana* is
a prostitute) no doubt owes something to the fact that it is a hot sauce, very
quickly made. It is also delicious.**

Drop the spaghetti into boiling salted water.

In a large frying pan, combine the oil, anchovies, garlic and chilli and fry for
1 minute. Add the tomatoes, olives and capers, and cook for a couple of minutes.
Taste and adjust the seasoning.

When the spaghetti is ready, drain and add to the frying pan together with
the parsley. Pour over the olio santo and stir-fry for 1 minute, using two forks
to lift the strands high up in the air so that they all get properly coated. Serve at
once. No cheese is served with this sauce.

Spaghetti alla pugliese

{ Spaghetti with tomatoes, anchovies and olives }

Serves 4

3 tbsp extra virgin olive oil

6 anchovy fillets, drained
and chopped, or 3 salted
anchovies, cleaned, rinsed
and chopped

500g/1lb 2oz fresh tomatoes,
peeled and seeded, or
canned plum tomatoes

2 garlic cloves,
finely chopped

salt

350g/12oz spaghetti

12 green olives, pitted

1 tbsp capers, rinsed

1 tbsp chopped flat-leaf
parsley

2 or 3 fresh basil leaves, torn
into pieces

3 tbsp olio santo (page 64)

This is one of many sauces that contain typical southern Italian ingredients – tomatoes, olives and anchovies – and I am sure it is one of the very best. It is the sauce I had in Puglia during one of my many trips to that blessed land of delicious food. Get an olive oil from Puglia, which has a particular and delicious almondy flavour.

This dish is also good cold, in which case you can add a little more olio santo – cold food needs stronger flavouring.

Heat the oil in a large frying pan, add the anchovies and cook for a couple of minutes, mashing them with a fork against the bottom of the pan. Add the tomatoes and garlic, and cook, uncovered, for about 15 minutes, or until the sauce has thickened. Taste and add salt.

While the sauce is cooking, cook the spaghetti in boiling salted water until al dente. When the pasta is ready, drain and transfer it to the frying pan. Stir-fry for 2–3 minutes, using two forks to separate the strands, and then add the olives, capers, parsley, basil and the olio santo. Mix well and serve at once.

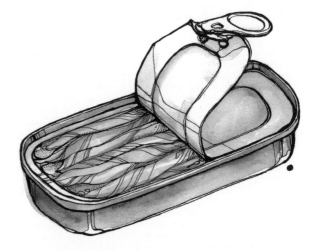

Pasta alla Norma

{ Pasta with fried aubergines and tomato sauce }

Serves 4

vegetable oil for deep-frying

350g/12oz aubergine
(eggplant), cut into
small cubes

salt

3 tbsp olive oil

2 garlic cloves, crushed

¼–½ tsp crushed dried
chillies, to taste

400g/14oz canned chopped
tomatoes

350g/12oz fusilli

3 tbsp extra virgin olive oil

a dozen fresh basil leaves,
torn into pieces

50g/1¾oz ricotta salata,
grated

This dish was created by the people of Catania for Vincenzo Bellini, composer of the opera *Norma*. The cheese used in Sicily is *ricotta salata* – dried salted ricotta – which is available from some Italian delis and online. If you cannot find it, use pecorino.

Most shapes of pasta, from bucatini to penne, are good with this sauce. Here I use fusilli.

Deep-fry the aubergine cubes in very hot vegetable oil, and when golden and just soft, lift them out with a slotted spoon and drain on kitchen paper. Sprinkle with salt.

Heat the olive oil in a large frying pan, add the garlic and chilli and cook for 1 minute. Add the tomatoes and a pinch or two of salt and cook over moderate heat for about 10–15 minutes, until almost all the liquid has evaporated.

While the tomato sauce is cooking, cook the fusilli in boiling salted water.

When the tomato sauce is thick, add the fried aubergine and mix together. When the pasta is ready, drain and turn it into the frying pan. Stir-fry for a minute or two, and then pour over the extra virgin olive oil, and sprinkle the basil leaves and the grated cheese over the top.

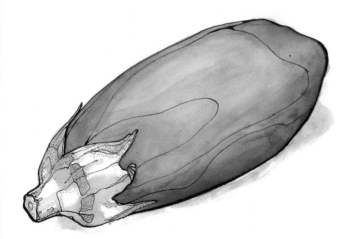

Orecchiette con i ceci

{ Orecchiette with chickpeas and leeks }

Serves 4

1 leek

6 tbsp extra virgin olive oil

350g/12oz orecchiette

3 tbsp chopped flat-leaf
parsley

½ red chilli, seeded and cut
into strips

225g/8oz/1 cup cooked
chickpeas, or drained
chickpeas from a can or
carton

salt and freshly ground
black pepper

This recipe adds a typical northern Italian vegetable, the leek, to a southern Italian sauce. It is a very successful combination of flavours. The best chickpeas to use are those you have cooked from scratch: soak dried chickpeas overnight and then simmer in water with an onion and 2 bay leaves until soft. Failing that, I use organic chickpeas from a carton, which I find much better than those in cans.

Keeping the root end intact, cut the leek lengthwise into very thin strips and then cut the strips to a length of about 10cm/4 inches. Wash and dry the strands.

Heat 1 tablespoon of the oil in a large frying pan. Throw in the leek strands and fry for about 3 minutes, until the strands are crisp. Remove them with a slotted spoon and drain on kitchen paper. Set aside.

Cook the pasta in boiling salted water.

While the pasta is cooking, pour the remaining oil into the frying pan, add the parsley and chilli and fry for 2 minutes, and then stir in the chickpeas. Season with salt and pepper to taste.

When the pasta is ready, drain and transfer it to the frying pan. Stir-fry the whole thing for a couple of minutes and then serve with the leeks sprinkled over the top.

Pennoni con le verdure arrostite

{ Pennoni with roasted vegetables }

Serves 4

4 ripe tomatoes, peeled and
thickly sliced

½ a large aubergine
(eggplant), about
150g/5½oz, thickly sliced

1 courgette (zucchini),
thickly sliced

1 red or yellow pepper, cut
into quarters, seeds and
cores removed

2 red onions, thickly sliced

6 tbsp extra virgin olive oil

1 garlic bulb

salt and freshly ground
black pepper

a good bunch of fresh basil
leaves, torn into
smallish pieces

350g/12oz pennoni

freshly grated Parmesan
cheese, to serve (optional)

Pennoni, or large penne, are good for this sauce: they match the size
of the vegetables. But you can use smaller penne or conchiglie, in fact
any large short pasta. This dish is also very good cold. In the autumn you
can make this with butternut squash, celeriac and small turnips instead
of the aubergine, courgette and pepper, but in that case you would not
serve this cold.

Preheat the oven to 200°C/400°F/gas mark 6.

Put the tomatoes, aubergine, courgette, pepper and onions in a roasting
pan. Pour 3 tablespoons of the oil over them. Break the garlic bulb into cloves,
removing the outer skin, and add the cloves to the vegetables. Season with salt
and plenty of pepper. Bake in the oven for about 40 minutes or until all the
vegetables are soft and slightly browned.

Put the remaining oil into a small bowl, add the basil leaves and beat well.

While the vegetables are roasting, cook the pasta in boiling salted water.
When it is al dente, drain and transfer to a serving bowl. Toss immediately with
the basil oil and then spoon all the vegetables over the top. Serve with grated
Parmesan, if you wish.

Lasagne al forno con le verdure
You can make a delicious pasta bake by layering the roasted vegetables with 10 sheets
of lasagne (previously cooked); finish with a layer of vegetables and 250g/9oz of
buffalo mozzarella, crumbled, and 250g/9oz of ricotta, also crumbled. Bake in a
preheated oven at 180°C/350°F/gas mark 4 for 30 minutes. Take the dish out of the
oven and leave to rest for about 5 minutes before serving.

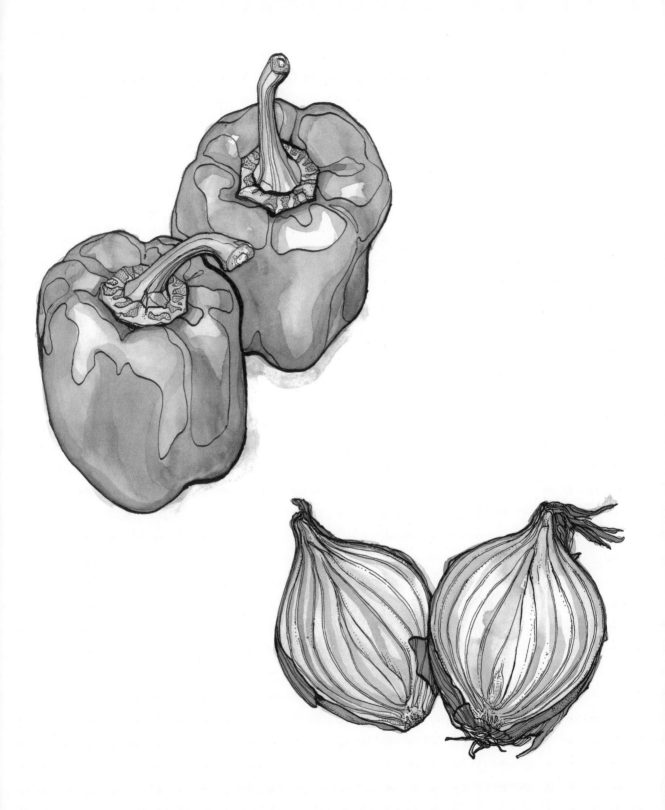

Pasta risottata in salsa

{ Pasta risotto in a tomato sauce }

Serves 4

6 tbsp extra virgin olive oil

1 garlic clove, chopped

250g/9oz fresh wild
mushrooms, cleaned and
roughly chopped

double quantity of plain
tomato sauce (page 72)

400g/14oz ditalini,
conchigliette or other
small pasta

salt

crushed dried chillies

3 tbsp chopped flat-leaf
parsley

I owe this recipe to Nigella Lawson, who, in her excellent book *Nigellissima*, brought this method of cooking pasta to my mind. Years ago, when we were staying in a B & B high up in the wilderness of the Calabrian mountains, I had a plate of ditalini floating in a red sauce speckled with brown bits and green blobs. It looked and tasted a little different from the usual pasta, so I asked the signora how it was made. 'Ma, Anna, can't you see? Just like your risotto.' The signora, who was the proprietor and the cook of the place, told me that it is a traditional dish of that part of the region. And now I read in *Nigellissima* that it is the *chiccoso* – the fashionable – way to cook pasta all over the peninsula (*plus ça change…*). Nigella makes the dish with pancetta and peas and it is delicious; I make it this way, as I first had it all those years ago in Calabria.

If you cannot find wild mushrooms, use chestnut (cremini) mushrooms and 30g/1oz of dried porcini soaked in hot water for 15–20 minutes.

Heat the oil in a large, heavy-bottomed saucepan, add the garlic and fry for 1 minute. Throw in the mushrooms and fry over high heat for about 5 minutes, until the mushrooms have released a lot of liquid.

Meanwhile, heat the tomato sauce in a pan and bring 1 litre/1¾ pints/4 cups of water to the boil in a kettle.

Add the pasta to the mushrooms, stir well and cook for 2–3 minutes, and then pour in half the tomato sauce. Bring slowly to the boil, stir well and add the rest of the sauce a little at the time as you would for a risotto, adding the next lot when the pasta looks dry. When all the tomato sauce has been added, begin to add the hot water from the kettle. It is impossible to state how much water you need to add. Just go slowly and add a little at a time, especially at the end, just as with risotto. Pasta cooked this way needs more time than boiled pasta, about 25 minutes. When the pasta is ready, taste and season with salt and chilli. Sprinkle with the parsley and serve.

Tajarin in bianco coi tartufi d'Alba

{ Tagliatelle with white truffles }

Serves 4

homemade tajarin
(pages 58–61) made with
200g/7oz Italian 00 flour
and 2 eggs, or 300g/10½oz
dried egg tagliatelle

1 small white truffle, about
25–30g/1oz

75g/2¾oz/5 tbsp unsalted
butter

50g/1¾oz Parmesan cheese,
grated, plus extra to serve

a grating of nutmeg

salt and freshly ground
black pepper

150ml/5fl oz/⅔ cup chicken
stock

Tajarin are the homemade tagliatelle of Piedmont. Here they are dressed in the best possible way, with butter, Parmesan and white truffle. I have not stated the quantity of white truffle you need, because it is a question of how much you want to spend. At the time of writing, white truffles cost about 150–200 euros per 100 grams. 25 grams are enough, but it is certainly not a cheap supper.

White truffles should not be cooked, while black truffles need a few minutes cooking to bring out their flavour.

You can use truffle cream, which is a mixture of white truffle and butter. Some makes are very good.

If you are making the pasta at home, follow the instructions for tagliatelle on page 61.

Gently clean the truffle with a brush and wipe with kitchen paper. I never wash my truffles, but you might find it difficult to get into all the nooks and crannies and prefer to give them a rinse under a cold tap.

Bring a large pot of salted water to the boil; when the water boils, slide in the tajerin. Give them a good stir and cook until al dente. If they are homemade, they will take only 2–3 minutes; if dried, follow the packet instructions.

Meanwhile, heat the butter in a saucepan over very low heat, add the Parmesan, a generous grating of nutmeg and plenty of pepper. Add the stock and boil to reduce slightly.

When the pasta is ready, drain, but do not overdrain. Turn the pasta into a warmed serving bowl and spoon over the butter sauce. Mix well and top the pasta with the regal truffle, very thinly sliced. Serve at once with grated Parmesan on the side.

Baked pasta dishes

Pasticci are made with various kinds of pasta and other ingredients.
The distinguishing characteristic of these dishes is that the ingredients
are prepared separately and then united for a final baking in the oven.
The most familiar types of pasticci are baked lasagne and macaroni cheese.
Very often they are topped with a béchamel sauce or a mixture of eggs and
cheese. Although definitely retro, pasticci are still often made in Italian
homes. So I decided to include those I liked best.

Pasticci are among the oldest pasta dishes. They were frequently served at
elegant dinners in the eighteenth century and at that time they were usually
known as *timballi* or *timpani*. Nowadays the words timballo and timpano are
seldom used, except when referring to dishes of the past.

Pasticci are substantial and nourishing dishes and they are particularly suitable
for parties, since they look beautiful and, if necessary, are easy to eat with just
a fork. The other advantage is that they can be prepared and assembled in
advance, even the day before. However, it is usually better to add the topping
of béchamel or whatever just before baking.

The pasta in the pasticci is usually cooked twice: first boiled in water, and
then baked in the oven. For this reason, when you boil your pasta, it should
be slightly undercooked and still a little hard to the bite. I use a large sauté
pan to boil lasagne, because I find it easier to fish the sheets out when done.

There are on the market dried lasagne that can be used without preboiling.
Frankly, I don't think the result is the same, but I leave it to you. However, if
you do not precook the lasagne, you must remember to add a little more liquid
when you layer them, and they need some 10 minutes longer in the oven.

Timpano di lasagne per il Duca d'Este

{ Baked lasagne with sole and prawns }

Serves 6–8

homemade lasagne
(pages 58–61) made with
300g/10½oz Italian 00 flour
and 3 eggs, or 20–22 sheets
of dried egg lasagne

2 litres/3½ pints/2 quarts
fish stock

250ml/9fl oz/1 cup dry white
wine

3 sole or other flat fish,
filleted

500g/1lb 2oz small raw
prawns (shrimp) in
their shells

125g/4½oz/½ cup unsalted
butter, plus extra for
the dish

1 garlic clove, lightly crushed

100g/3½oz/generous ¾ cup
Italian 00 flour

1½ tbsp tomato purée (paste)

1 tbsp paprika

salt and freshly ground
black pepper

bunch of dill, chopped

50g/1¾oz Parmesan cheese,
grated

4 tbsp dried breadcrumbs

I found this recipe in *Libro novo nel qual s'insegna il modo d'ordinar banchetti* – A new book on how to give banquets – by Christoforo di Messisbugo, who in the sixteenth century was steward to the Dukes d'Este of Ferrara, one of the great Renaissance families. In this splendid dish Messisbugo uses the sole from the nearby Adriatic, which have a unique and delicate flavour.

If you are making the pasta at home, follow the instructions on pages 58–61. Set the raw sheets of lasagne aside, spread on clean tea towels.

Bring the fish stock and wine to the boil in a large sauté pan, slide in the fish fillets and simmer for 2 minutes. Using a fish slice, lift out the fillets and remove the dark skin. Set aside.

Plunge the prawns into the stock and boil gently for 3 minutes. Scoop them out and, as soon as they are cool enough to handle, shell them and set aside.

Strain the fish stock and measure about 1.5 litres/2½ pints/1¼ quarts. Return this measured stock to the pan and keep it just simmering.

Preheat the oven to 180°C/350°F/gas mark 4. Generously butter a 30 x 20cm/12 x 8 inch lasagne dish.

In a heavy-bottomed saucepan melt 100g/3½oz/scant ½ cup of the butter with the garlic clove and cook for 1 minute. Fish out and discard the garlic, add the flour and cook, stirring constantly, until all the flour has been absorbed. Now mix in the tomato purée and the paprika and cook for a minute. Remove the pan from the heat and gradually add about 1 litre/1¾ pints/4 cups of the fish stock, stirring constantly. Put the pan back over low heat and bring to the boil. Slowly add more stock until the sauce has the consistency of pouring cream, and simmer for 5 minutes. Add salt and pepper to taste. Set aside.

Cook the lasagne in boiling salted water a few sheets at a time; if homemade, they will take no more than 1–2 minutes; if dried, start testing 2 minutes before the time suggested on the packet. When they are still just a little hard to the bite, lift them out and lay them on clean tea towels while you cook the rest.

Assemble the dish. Spread 2–3 tablespoons of the sauce over the bottom of the dish and cover with lasagne sheets, cutting them up to fit. Do not leave any gaps; overlap the lasagne if necessary. Spread over 2–3 tablespoons of the sauce and then lay the fish fillets on the sauce, side by side. Now cover with lasagne, then some more of the sauce, then the prawns, and finish with a layer of lasagne.

Mix the dill into the remaining sauce and spread the sauce all over the pasta. Mix the Parmesan with the breadcrumbs and sprinkle all over the top. Dot with the remaining butter and then bake for about 30 minutes. Take the dish out of the oven and leave to rest for at least 5 minutes before serving.

Timballo di lasagne alla Montefeltro

{ Baked lasagne with ham and cheeses }

Serves 6–8

homemade lasagne (pages 58–61) made with 300g/10½oz Italian 00 flour and 3 eggs, or 18–20 sheets of dried egg lasagne

200g/7oz buffalo mozzarella, diced

200g/7oz Bel Paese cheese, diced

250g/9oz cooked ham or tongue, cut into thin short strips

150ml/5fl oz/⅔ cup double (heavy) cream

salt and ground black pepper

100g/3½oz Parmesan cheese, grated

100g/3½oz/scant ½ cup unsalted butter, plus extra for the dish

béchamel sauce (p. 74) made with 600ml milk, 50g butter and 40–45g flour, flavoured with nutmeg

4 tbsp dried breadcrumbs

This dish was allegedly served at the court of the Duke of Montefeltro in his palace in Urbino. Federico da Montefeltro was perhaps the greatest of all Renaissance men: a great soldier, statesman, humanist, man of letters and patron of the arts. His palace stands witness to his artistic taste, and this dish proves that he was also a connoisseur of gastronomic delights.

If you are making the pasta at home, follow the instructions on pages 58–61. Cook the lasagne in boiling salted water a few sheets at a time; if homemade, they will take no more than 1–2 minutes; if dried, start testing 2 minutes before the time suggested on the packet. When they are still just a little hard to the bite, lift them out and lay them on clean tea towels while you cook the rest.

Preheat the oven to 180°C/350°F/gas mark 4. Generously butter a 30 x 20cm/12 x 8 inch lasagne dish.

Combine the diced mozzarella, Bel Paese, ham and cream. Add seasoning to taste. Cover the bottom of the lasagne dish with a layer of lasagne and spoon over it 2–3 tablespoons of the béchamel. Spoon over a few tablespoons of the ham and cheese mixture, sprinkle with some grated Parmesan and dot with some of the butter. Repeat, omitting the béchamel, to make three or four layers, until you have used all the ingredients, finishing with lasagne.

Cover with the béchamel, sprinkle with the remaining Parmesan mixed with the dried breadcrumbs, and then dot with the remaining butter. Bake for about 30 minutes, or until the top is beautifully golden. Take the dish out of the oven and leave to rest for 5 minutes before serving.

Timpano di lasagne di Bartolomeo Scappi

{ Baked lasagne with prosciutto and mozzarella }

Serves 4

homemade lasagne
  (pages 58–61) made with
  200g/7oz Italian 00 flour
  and 2 eggs, or about 9–10
  sheets of dried egg lasagne

3 eggs

200ml/7fl oz/generous ¾ cup
  double (heavy) cream

100g/3½oz Parmesan cheese,
  grated

salt and freshly ground
  black pepper

a generous grating of nutmeg

200g/7oz prosciutto

250g/9oz buffalo mozzarella,
  crumbled into small pieces

a few leaves of fresh sage,
  torn into small pieces

1 white truffle, brushed clean
  (optional)

50g/1¾oz/4 tbsp unsalted
  butter, plus extra for the tin

This is a recipe by Bartolomeo Scappi, who was chef to Pope Pius V in the sixteenth century. It is a most delicate and delicious dish, but rather expensive, because of the truffle. You can omit the truffle, but the taste would certainly not be the same.

If you are making the pasta at home, follow the instructions on pages 58–61. Set the raw sheets of lasagne aside, spread on clean tea towels.

Butter a loaf tin with a capacity of 1 litre/1¾ pints/4 cups. Line it with baking parchment and butter the parchment. Preheat the oven to 180°C/350°F/gas mark 4.

Cook the lasagne in boiling salted water a few sheets at a time; if homemade, they will take no more than 1–2 minutes; if dried, start testing 2 minutes before the time suggested on the packet. When they are still just a little hard to the bite, lift them out and lay them on clean tea towels while you cook the rest.

In a bowl lightly beat together the eggs, cream and about two-thirds of the Parmesan. Season with salt, pepper and nutmeg.

Now you can assemble the pasticcio. Use the prosciutto to line the prepared tin, laying the slices across the tin and slightly overlapping them, so that the bottom and sides of the tin are completely lined. Cover the prosciutto with a layer of lasagne. Then spoon 2–3 tablespoons of the egg mixture over the lasagne, dot with a few pieces of mozzarella, a few pieces of sage and a grating of truffle, if you are using it. Every now and then, dot with butter. Cover with lasagne and then spoon over some more of the egg mixture, the mozzarella, sage and truffle. Build up the timpano, finishing with a layer of lasagne. Dot with the remaining butter and sprinkle with the remaining Parmesan. If there are any overhanging bits of prosciutto, fold them over the top and then cover the top with a sheet of buttered foil.

Put the loaf tin into a roasting pan and pour some boiling water into the roasting pan to come about three-quarters of the way up the loaf tin. Place in the oven and bake for about 30 minutes.

Take the roasting pan out of the oven and lift out the loaf tin. Leave to rest for 5 minutes and then put an oval dish over the tin and turn them upside down. The timpano should fall onto the dish. Peel off the baking parchment and serve.

I like to serve this surrounded by stewed mushrooms or by peas cooked in stock and butter.

Timpano del Cardinale Alberoni

{ Baked pasta with prawns and mushrooms }

Serves 6–8

6 tbsp olive oil

500g/1lb 2oz chestnut (cremini) mushrooms, finely sliced

1 garlic clove, finely sliced

500g/1lb 2oz peeled prawns (shrimp)

6 tbsp dry Marsala

500g/1lb 2oz farfalle or mafalde

300ml/10fl oz/1¼ cups double (heavy) cream

2 eggs and 1 egg yolk

100g/3½oz Parmesan cheese, grated

béchamel sauce (page 74) made with 750ml milk, 75g unsalted butter and 60g flour

2 tbsp dried breadcrumbs

30g/1oz/2 tbsp unsalted butter, plus extra for the dish

This pasta bake is supposed to have been created by Cardinal Giulio Alberoni from Piacenza in Emilia; he was a distinguished eighteenth-century soldier, churchman and, judging by this recipe, gourmet. I like farfalle or mafalde for this dish, two pasta shapes that certainly didn't exist in Alberoni's time, but they are perfect here.

Heat the oil in a sauté pan, add the mushrooms and garlic and sauté for about 8 minutes, turning them over frequently. Add the prawns and cook for 2–3 minutes. Pour in the Marsala and cook briskly for 2 minutes. Remove the pan from the heat and set aside.

Drop the pasta into rapidly boiling salted water.

Preheat the oven to 180°C/350°F/gas mark 4. Butter a shallow baking dish.

In a bowl, mix together the cream, eggs, egg yolk and half the Parmesan.

When the pasta is just al dente, drain and return it to the pan in which it has cooked. Add the mushroom and prawn mixture and the cream mixture. Mix thoroughly and then ladle the pasta into the baking dish.

Spread the béchamel over the top and sprinkle with the remaining Parmesan mixed with the breadcrumbs. Dot with butter and bake for about 30 minutes, until golden. Take the dish out of the oven and leave to rest for 5 minutes before serving.

Torta settecentesca di vermicelli e pomodori

{ Baked vermicelli with tomatoes }

Serves 6–8

1.25kg/2lb 12oz large fresh tomatoes, peeled

salt and freshly ground black pepper

500g/1lb 2oz vermicelli or spaghettini (thin spaghetti)

125ml/4fl oz/½ cup extra virgin olive oil

100g/3½oz/1 cup dried breadcrumbs

3 garlic cloves, finely chopped

½ tsp crushed dried chillies

6 salted anchovies, cleaned and rinsed, or 12 anchovy fillets, drained, chopped

500g/1lb 2oz buffalo mozzarella, sliced

50g/1¾oz Parmesan cheese, grated

about 24 fresh basil leaves, torn into pieces

This is an eighteenth-century recipe from Naples, which I found in my mother's recipe book, a book that contains quite a few recipes from her Neapolitan grandmother. It is an easy, attractive and delicious dish, but it demands the finest ingredients: the best tomatoes, good buffalo mozzarella and the best olive oil. I make this in a round earthenware dish, just because it looks beautiful, but a lasagne dish will do.

Put the peeled tomatoes in the fridge for at least 30 minutes to firm up. Cut each tomato horizontally into slices, lay them on a board and sprinkle with salt. Leave for 30 minutes to bring out the flavour.

Cook the spaghetti in boiling salted water; when it is ready but still slightly undercooked, drain and dress immediately with about 2 tablespoons of the oil.

While the pasta is cooking, heat 2 tablespoons of the oil in a frying pan, add the breadcrumbs, garlic, chilli and anchovies and fry for about 5 minutes, turning the mixture over frequently and squashing the anchovies against the pan. Set aside.

Preheat the oven to 200°C/400°F/gas mark 6. Grease a shallow baking dish with 2 tablespoons of the oil, and cover the bottom with the inner slices of the tomatoes. Spread over them half the mozzarella, half the breadcrumb mixture, half the Parmesan and half the basil, and season with salt and pepper. Spread the cooked spaghetti over this layer and then cover with the ends of the tomatoes, round side up, the remaining mozzarella, breadcrumb mixture, basil and Parmesan. Carefully drizzle the remaining oil over the top and bake for about 30 minutes.

Take the dish out of the oven and leave to rest for about 5 minutes before serving.

Pasticcio di tagliatelle alla boscaiola

{ Baked tagliatelle with mushrooms and eggs }

Serves 6

homemade pasta
  (pages 58–61) made with
  400g/14oz Italian 00 flour,
  2 eggs, about 125ml/4fl oz/
  ½ cup water and 1 tsp salt,
  or 400g/14oz dried egg
  tagliatelle

2 or 3 slices white bread,
  crusts removed

125ml/4fl oz/½ cup whole
  milk

30g/1oz dried porcini

4 tbsp olive oil

350g/12oz chestnut
  (cremini) mushrooms,
  chopped

2 whole garlic cloves

3 eggs

salt and freshly ground
  black pepper

75g/2¾oz/5 tbsp unsalted
  butter, plus extra for
  the dish

100g/3½oz Gruyère cheese,
  finely sliced

100g/3½oz Bel Paese cheese,
  finely sliced

50g/1¾oz Parmesan cheese,
  grated

125ml/4fl oz/½ cup double
  (heavy) cream

The tagliatelle for this pasticcio are made with a less rich dough than usual, some of the eggs being replaced with water. If you prefer, make the usual dough or use dried egg tagliatelle.

If you are making the pasta at home, follow the instructions for tagliatelle on pages 58–61, adding the water to the eggs before mixing in the flour. It is difficult to give the exact amount of water, but the dough should be elastic, smooth and compact, like that made with eggs, although it should not be rolled out as thin. Leave the rolled-out dough to dry.

While the pasta dough is drying, soak the bread in the milk and soak the dried porcini in 125ml/4fl oz/½ cup of hot water for about 15 minutes. When the porcini are soft, lift them out of the water and chop them. Reserve the liquid.

Preheat the oven to 180°C/350°F/gas mark 4. Generously butter a baking dish.

Heat the oil in a frying pan, add the porcini, fresh mushrooms and garlic cloves and sauté for 15 minutes, stirring frequently. Remove the garlic and transfer the mushrooms and their juices to a bowl. Break in the eggs and mix thoroughly. Squeeze the milk out of the bread and add to the mushroom mixture, together with salt and pepper to taste. Mash it all up with a fork and mix well. Set aside.

If you are making your own tagliatelle, cut the rolled-out pasta dough into strands about 8mm wide, or use the broad cutting blades of your pasta machine. Cook the tagliatelle in boiling salted water; if you are using homemade tagliatelle, drain it 1 minute after the water returns to the boil. If using dried tagliatelle, drain when it is very al dente. Toss with half the butter.

Transfer half the tagliatelle to the baking dish, spread over the mushroom and egg mixture, and cover with the sliced cheeses. Sprinkle with half of the Parmesan and then cover with the remaining tagliatelle. Pour over the cream, sprinkle with the remaining Parmesan, and dot with the rest of the butter. Bake for 30 minutes, or until the top is slightly golden. Take the dish out of the oven and leave to rest for a few minutes before serving.

Timpano di maccheroni alla Pompadour

{ Baked macaroni with chicken and prosciutto }

Serves 8

500g/1lb 2oz boneless loin of
  pork in one piece

125g/4½oz/½ cup unsalted
  butter, plus extra for
  the dish

3 tbsp olive oil

2 sprigs of rosemary, about
  5cm/2 inches long

125ml/4fl oz/½ cup dry
  white wine

salt and freshly ground
  black pepper

500g/1lb 2oz skinless,
  boneless chicken breasts

300g/10½oz prosciutto

1 small black or white truffle,
  brushed clean and sliced
  very thin (optional)

750g/1lb 10oz macaroni
  or penne

100g/3½oz Parmesan cheese,
  grated

4 egg yolks

300ml/10fl oz/1¼ cups
  double (heavy) cream

1 tsp ground cinnamon

3 tbsp dried white
  breadcrumbs

An eighteenth-century Neapolitan recipe by the Prince of Francavilla. This nobleman created quite a few excellent recipes; he used to dictate them to his secretary, Vincenzo Corrado, who revised and published them in a book called *Il Cuoco Galante*, which became a bestseller. I have been unable to find out why this dish – originally made with capon breast – is dedicated to Madame de Pompadour, the mistress of Louis XV of France.

Choose a heavy-bottomed casserole into which the pork will fit snugly. In it, heat 15g/½oz/1 tbsp of the butter, the oil and rosemary, and when the butter begins to colour, add the pork and cook until brown on all sides. Add the wine, turn up the heat to reduce by half and then turn the heat down so that the liquid is just simmering. Season with salt and pepper and cover the pan, putting the lid just slightly askew to allow some evaporation. Cook for about 40–45 minutes, until the pork is just cooked, which depends on how thick the meat is (test by piercing with a skewer); add a little hot water if necessary so that the pork is never cooking without liquid.

Lift out the meat and set aside for another meal; you only need the juices. Add about 100ml/3½fl oz/scant ½ cup of hot water to the casserole and bring to the boil, scraping the bottom of the pan with a spoon to release the cooking residue. Measure the liquid: you need about 125ml/4fl oz/½ cup. If there is too much, boil to reduce it some more; if too little, add a little hot water.

Heat 30g/1oz/2 tbsp of the remaining butter in a frying pan and sauté the chicken breasts, turning once or twice, until cooked, about 15–20 minutes, depending on how thick they are. Season with salt and pepper and add a little hot water as they cook.

Finely chop the chicken breasts and the prosciutto. I do this by hand because I find the food processor tends to reduce them to a mush. Transfer the mixture to a bowl and add the juices from cooking the pork and chicken breasts, and then the truffle, if using it. Taste and adjust the seasoning.

Preheat oven to 200°C/400°F/gas mark 6. Generously butter a baking dish.

Cook the pasta in boiling salted water. When it is just al dente, drain and turn it into the bowl with the meat mixture. Add the remaining butter and half the Parmesan and mix thoroughly, using two forks – forks are more efficient at separating all the different elements. Spoon this mixture into the baking dish.

In another bowl mix together the egg yolks, cream, half of the remaining Parmesan, cinnamon and a generous amount of pepper. Spoon this mixture over the pasta, sprinkle with the remaining Parmesan mixed with the breadcrumbs and bake for 20–30 minutes, or until a golden crust has formed on the top. Take the dish out of the oven and leave to rest for at least 5 minutes before serving.

Pasticcio di pasta alla napoletana

{ Baked pasta with tomato and mozzarella }

Serves 4–6

a little butter for the dish

350g/12oz short pasta, such as penne

125ml/4fl oz/½ cup extra virgin olive oil

double quantity of Neapolitan tomato sauce (page 72)

250g/9oz buffalo mozzarella, sliced

50g/1¾oz pecorino cheese, grated

3 tbsp soft white breadcrumbs

30g/1oz fresh flat-leaf parsley, coarsely chopped

9 or 10 fresh basil leaves, torn into pieces

2 tbsp dried oregano

½ tsp crushed dried chillies

salt and freshly ground black pepper

This is a classic baked pasta dish of southern Italy. You can use any short pasta.

Preheat the oven to 180°C/350°F/gas mark 4. Butter a baking dish.

Cook the pasta in boiling salted water. As soon as it is al dente, drain it and toss with 2 tablespoons of the oil.

Spoon a third of the pasta into the buttered dish. Cover with a third of the tomato sauce, a third of the mozzarella, a third of the pecorino, a third of the breadcrumbs and a third of the herbs. Season with chilli, salt and pepper and sprinkle with 1 tablespoon of olive oil. Repeat to make two more layers, ending with a sprinkling of pecorino and all the remaining olive oil. Cover with foil and bake for about 20 minutes. Remove the foil and bake for an additional 10 minutes. Take the pasticcio out of oven and leave to rest for a few minutes before serving.

Pasta con le sarde

{ Pasta with fresh sardines }

Serves 4

50g/1¾oz/⅓ cup sultanas
(golden raisins)

50g/1¾oz/⅓ cup pine nuts

5 tbsp extra virgin olive oil,
plus extra for the dish

1 onion, very finely sliced

salt and freshly ground
black pepper

75g/2¾oz fennel leaf tops
(the feathery fronds)

2 salted anchovies, cleaned
and rinsed, or 4 anchovy
fillets, drained

500g/1lb 2oz fresh sardines,
filleted

1 tsp fennel seeds

350/12oz rigatoni or penne

This is one of the greatest combinations of pasta and fish. It comes from Sicily, as do many of the best pasta dishes. In Sicily the sauce is made with wild fennel, which is slightly different from cultivated fennel bulb and has thick and plentiful fronds and a stronger flavour. If you cannot get enough of the feathery leaf tops from fennel bulb, make up the weight with very finely sliced fennel bulb mixed with some flat-leaf parsley.

Soak the sultanas in warm water for 10 minutes. Drain and dry with kitchen paper. Dry-fry the pine nuts in a cast-iron or heavy-bottomed pan for 3–4 minutes to release the aroma.

Heat 3 tablespoons of the oil in a frying pan, add the onion and a little salt and sauté gently, stirring frequently, for about 10 minutes, until softened. Mix in the sultanas and pine nuts and continue cooking for a minute or two. Set aside.

Blanch the fennel in a large saucepan of boiling salted water for 1 minute. Using a slotted spoon, lift the fennel fronds out of the water and drain in a colander, then dry them with kitchen paper. Reserve the cooking water.

Chop the fennel fronds and add to the onion mixture. Cook over low heat for 10 minutes, adding a couple of tablespoons of the reserved fennel water whenever the mixture seems dry.

Preheat the oven to 200°C/400°F/gas mark 6. Grease a deep baking dish with olive oil.

Chop the anchovies and about half the sardines and add to the onion mixture, along with the fennel seeds and a generous grinding of pepper. Cook for 5–7 minutes, stirring frequently and adding more fennel water whenever necessary. Taste and adjust the seasoning.

While the sauce is cooking, bring the remaining fennel water back to a rapid boil, adding more boiling water if necessary, and cook the pasta until it is just al dente. Drain the pasta and tip it into the sauce. Cook for a minute or two, stirring constantly, and then transfer it to the baking dish.

Lay the remaining sardine fillets over the pasta, drizzle with the remaining oil, cover with foil and bake for 10–15 minutes, or until the sardines are done. Take the dish out of the oven and leave to rest for a few minutes before serving.

Pasticcio di fusilli e melanzane

{ Baked fusilli and aubergine }

Serves 6

500g/1lb 2oz aubergines
  (eggplants)

salt and freshly ground
  black pepper

double quantity of plain
  tomato sauce (page 72)

5 tbsp extra virgin olive oil

2–3 tbsp dried breadcrumbs

vegetable oil for deep-frying

350g/12oz fusilli, penne or
  elbow macaroni

350g/12oz buffalo
  mozzarella, sliced

30g/1oz pecorino or
  Parmesan cheese, grated

This is a simpler variation of the Sicilian dish called pasta 'ncasciata, in which slices of fried aubergine line a cake tin filled with short pasta dressed with tomato sauce and mozzarella.

Slice the aubergines into rounds, put them in a colander and toss with 2 tablespoons of salt. Set aside while you make the tomato sauce.

Preheat the oven to 180°C/350°F/gas mark 4. Brush a baking dish with a little olive oil.

Heat 2 tablespoons of the olive oil in a small pan and fry the breadcrumbs until golden. Set aside.

Rinse the aubergine slices and dry thoroughly on kitchen paper. Deep-fry them in very hot vegetable oil for about 5 minutes – in batches if necessary. When they are golden brown, lift them out with a slotted spoon and drain on kitchen paper.

Cook the pasta in boiling salted water. When it is just al dente, drain and tip it back into the pan, and then mix in the tomato sauce.

Cover the bottom of the baking dish with a layer of pasta, then add a layer of aubergine and a layer of sliced mozzarella. Add a few twists of freshly ground pepper. Repeat these layers until all the ingredients are used up, ending with a layer of mozzarella. Sprinkle with the grated cheese and the fried breadcrumbs, and pour over the remaining oil. Cover with foil and bake for 30 minutes, removing the foil after 15 minutes. Take the dish out of the oven and leave to rest for a few minutes before serving.

Variation
Use cooked, drained lasagne sheets instead of fusilli. In this case, starting from the bottom, the layers would be: lasagne, aubergine, tomato sauce, mozzarella, finishing with the mozzarella and grated cheese.

Pasticcio di penne, pollo e fegatini in salsa di funghi

{ Baked pasta, chicken and chicken livers in a mushroom sauce }

Serves 6

15g/½oz dried porcini

4 tbsp olive oil

75g/2¾oz/5 tbsp unsalted butter, plus extra for the dish

50g/1¾oz unsmoked pancetta, chopped

1 shallot, finely chopped

1 very small celery stalk with its leaves, finely chopped

½ small carrot, finely chopped

4–5 sprigs of fresh thyme, leaves only

100g/3½oz chicken livers, any bits of fat removed, coarsely chopped

200–250g/7–9oz roasted chicken, cut into small pieces

4 tbsp dry Marsala, vermouth or dry sherry

salt and freshly ground black pepper

150g/5½oz chestnut (cremini) mushrooms, chopped

2 egg yolks

300ml/10fl oz/1¼ cups double (heavy) cream

75g/2¾oz Parmesan cheese, grated

500g/1lb 2oz penne or elbow macaroni

2–3 tbsp dried breadcrumbs

This is a very good way to finish the leftovers from your roasted chicken. You can also use any large shapes of pasta, such as ditaloni or conchiglie.

Put the porcini in a bowl, cover with boiling water and set aside.

Heat half the oil and half the butter in a sauté pan. When hot, add the pancetta, the shallot, celery, carrot and thyme and sauté for about 10 minutes, stirring frequently, until the vegetables have softened. Throw in the chicken livers and cook over high heat for 3 minutes, stirring constantly. Add the chicken pieces and then splash with the Marsala and season with salt and pepper. Cook for 2 minutes, stirring the whole time. Remove the pan from the heat, cover to keep warm and set aside.

Preheat the oven to 180°C/350°F/gas mark 4. Butter a baking dish. Drain the porcini, reserving the liquid, and chop the bigger pieces.

Heat the remaining oil and half of the remaining butter in a large frying pan. When hot, throw in the porcini, fry for a minute and then add the fresh mushrooms and fry for 5 minutes or so. Season with salt and pepper and turn down the heat. Cook gently for 8 minutes, gradually adding the reserved porcini liquid. At the end the mushrooms should swim in quite a bit of liquid; they are stewed rather than sautéed.

Lightly beat the egg yolks in a bowl, add the cream and Parmesan and a good grinding of pepper and beat well with a fork.

While the mushrooms are cooking, cook the penne in boiling salted water. When just al dente, drain, reserving a cupful of the water. Transfer the pasta to the frying pan with the mushrooms and mix thoroughly.

Tip half of the pasta into the baking dish, cover with the chicken liver mixture and then top with the remaining pasta. Dot little pieces of butter here and there among the penne, keeping some butter for the top. Add 3–4 tablespoons of the reserved pasta water. Pour the cream mixture all over the pasta, beating the mixture briskly with a fork while you pour. Sprinkle with the breadcrumbs and dot with butter. Cover with foil and bake for 15 minutes, then remove the foil and continue baking for 5–10 minutes, until a lovely golden crust has formed. Take the dish out of the oven and leave to rest for about 5 minutes before serving.

Pasticcio di Garibaldi

{ Pasticcio of penne with beef and mozzarella }

Serves 6–8

ragù alla napoletana
  (page 71)

500g/1lb 2oz penne,
  macaroni, or other
  short pasta

250g/9oz/1¾ cups shelled
  fresh peas or frozen peas

50g/1¾oz/4 tbsp unsalted
  butter, plus extra for
  the dish

50g/1¾oz/4 tbsp Parmesan
  cheese, grated

250g/9oz buffalo mozzarella,
  sliced

2 tbsp extra virgin olive oil

salt and freshly ground
  black pepper

This dish was allegedly created for the homesick Garibaldi when he was fighting in South America in the 1840s. Garibaldi or not, this dish is very good. You can use cow's milk mozzarella instead of buffalo's, but to a slight detriment of the dish. You will need to make the ragù alla napoletana one or two days in advance.

Make the ragù one or two days in advance and, when cold, put it in the fridge. When you want to cook the dish, lift the meat out of its sauce and cut off about 350g/12oz, which is all you need for this dish. Keep the rest of the meat and 3–4 tablespoons of the sauce for another meal. Cut the meat into thin slices and then shred it. Put it into a pan with 500–600ml/18–20fl oz/2¼ –2½ cups of the sauce and place over low heat to warm through.

Drop the penne into a pan of rapidly boiling salted water. Meanwhile, put the peas in a small pan with 100ml/3½fl oz/scant ½ cup of water, 15g/½oz/ 1 tablespoon of the butter and ½ teaspoon of salt, cover the pan and cook until tender.

Preheat the oven to 180°C/350°F/gas mark 4. Butter a large baking dish.

Drain the pasta when just slightly undercooked and return it to the pan in which it has cooked. Mix in the remaining butter, the peas with all their liquid and the ragù. Mix well, add the Parmesan and mix again.

Spoon the pasta into the baking dish. Place the sliced mozzarella neatly on the top and sprinkle with the olive oil, a little salt and a lot of pepper.

Bake for about 20–25 minutes, until the mozzarella is bubbling. Take the pasticcio out of the oven and leave to rest for 3–5 minutes before serving.

Pasticcio di lasagne alla Saint-Martin

{ Pasticcio of lasagne with cheeses and mushrooms }

Serves 6–8

homemade lasagne
  (pages 58–61) made with
  300g/10½oz Italian 00 flour
  and 3 eggs, or 16–18 sheets
  of dried egg lasagne

4 tbsp olive oil

500g/1lb 2oz wild
  mushrooms, cleaned and
  thinly sliced

1 garlic clove, finely chopped

5–6 tbsp whole milk

2 tsp lemon juice

salt and freshly ground
  black pepper

200g/7oz mozzarella, sliced

200g/7oz fontina cheese,
  sliced

100g/3½oz/½ cup ricotta,
  crumbled

50g/1¾oz Parmesan cheese,
  grated

150g/5½oz/generous ½ cup
  unsalted butter, plus extra
  for the dish

125ml/4fl oz/½ cup double
  (heavy) cream

This recipe is from Valle d'Aosta, where mushrooms are plentiful in the woods and the local cheeses are rich and sweet. Ideally this dish should be made with wild mushrooms, but if they are not in season, use chestnut (cremini) mushrooms plus 40g/1½oz of dried porcini (which must be soaked in hot water for 15–20 minutes before use). Fontina cheese is available in some supermarkets and in most Italian delicatessens. It is by far the best cheese for this dish, although Gruyère is a good substitute.

If you are making the pasta at home, follow the instructions on pages 58–61. Leave the raw lasagne sheets on clean tea towels while you prepare the mushrooms.

Heat the oil in a sauté pan, add the mushrooms and garlic and cook over high heat for 5 minutes, stirring very frequently. Turn down the heat, add the milk and continue cooking for 10 minutes or until the mushrooms are tender, which depends on the species. Add the lemon juice, salt and pepper, mix and set aside.

Preheat the oven to 180°C/350°F/gas mark 4. Generously butter a 30 x 20cm/12 x 8 inch lasagne dish.

Cook the lasagne in boiling salted water a few sheets at a time; if homemade, they will take no more than 1–2 minutes; if dried, start testing 2 minutes before the time suggested on the packet. When they are still just a little hard to the bite, lift them out and lay them on clean tea towels while you cook the rest.

Cover the bottom of the lasagne dish with a layer of lasagne, without overlapping the sheets too much. Spread over about a third of the sliced cheeses, a third of the ricotta and a third of the mushrooms with their juices. Sprinkle with some Parmesan, salt and pepper and dot with about 30g/1oz/2 tbsp of the butter. Repeat these layers twice more, until all the ingredients are used up, finishing with a layer of lasagne.

Top with the remaining butter and Parmesan. Pour the cream all over the top, cover with foil and bake for 15 minutes. Remove the foil and continue baking for 15 minutes, until the top is golden. Take the pasticcio out of the oven and leave to rest for 5 minutes before serving.

Rigatoni gratinati ai cinque formaggi

{ Baked rigatoni with five cheeses }

Serves 4–5

350g/12oz rigatoni

125g/4½oz/½ cup unsalted butter, plus extra for the dish

100g/3½oz Grana Padano or Parmesan cheese, grated

100g/3½oz fontina cheese, thinly sliced

100g/3½oz Bel Paese cheese, thinly sliced

100g/3½oz Taleggio cheese, thinly sliced

150g/5½oz Gruyère cheese. thinly sliced

béchamel sauce (page 74), flavoured with nutmeg

2 tbsp dried breadcrumbs

This recipe is from Lombardy, the region where the best cow's milk cheeses are produced. It is a dish similar to – though far richer than – macaroni cheese, well known in England and the United States since the nineteenth century.

Preheat the oven to 180°C/350°F/gas mark 4. Generously butter a baking dish.

Make the béchamel sauce, following the instructions on page 74.

Cook the rigatoni in boiling salted water until it is just al dente. Drain the pasta and toss it with 90g/2¾oz/6 tablespoons of the butter and half of the Grana Padano.

Spoon half of the pasta into the baking dish. Lay the cheese slices over the pasta and then cover with the remaining pasta. Spread over the béchamel sauce, sprinkle with the remaining grated cheese mixed with the breadcrumbs, and dot with the remaining butter. Bake for 25–30 minutes, or until the top is golden. Take the dish out of the oven and leave to rest for a few minutes before serving.

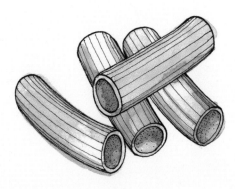

Pasticcio di fusilli e peperoni arrostiti

{ Baked fusilli and roasted peppers }

Serves 4

4 large yellow and
  red peppers

4 tbsp olive oil, plus extra for
  the dish

2 garlic cloves, crushed

¼ tsp crushed dried chillies

2 sprigs of marjoram

300g/10½oz fusilli

3 tbsp soft breadcrumbs

a dozen pitted black olives,
  cut into strips

1 tbsp capers, rinsed

75g/2¾oz ricotta salata,
  grated

2 tbsp olio santo (page 64)

salt and freshly ground
  black pepper

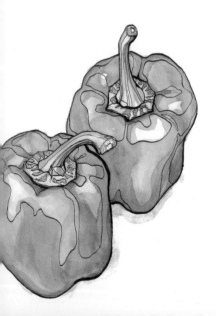

In this recipe from Calabria, the toe of the Italian boot, ricotta salata is the cheese used. It is a kind of dried ricotta made from sheep's milk, a tangy, slightly salted cheese, full of flavour. It is available from Italian delicatessens and online. If you use it, be careful when adding salt to the sauce. If you cannot find it, use mature pecorino instead.

If possible, start making this at least a day in advance to allow the peppers to pick up the flavour of the marinade.

Put the peppers on a direct flame or under the grill and char the skin on all sides. Be careful not to burn them too much, or you will not have much left. Put them in a bowl, cover with clingfilm and set aside. When they are cool, peel them very carefully, and then wipe them with kitchen paper. Cut each pepper into quarters, discard the seeds and white ribs and cut lengthwise into small strips, the same length as the fusilli. Put the strips in a container, add 1 tablespoon of oil, the crushed garlic cloves, the chilli and the sprigs of marjoram and place the container in the fridge.

Preheat the oven to 180°C/350°F/gas mark 4. Grease a shallow baking dish with a little olive oil.

Drop the fusilli into rapidly boiling salted water.

While the pasta is cooking, sauté the breadcrumbs in the remaining oil for 3–4 minutes, stirring very frequently, until crisp, and then mix in the olives and capers. Set aside.

When the pasta is just al dente, drain and return it to the pan in which it has cooked. Add the peppers with their marinade, the ricotta salata and 1 tablespoon of the olio santo. Mix well and season to taste.

Spoon the pasta into the baking dish, sprinkle with the breadcrumb mixture and bake for about 20 minutes, until a nice crust has formed on the top. Just before serving, pour over the remaining olio santo.

Pizzoccheri

{ Buckwheat tagliatelle with Savoy cabbage and potatoes }

Serves 6

200g/7oz/generous 1½ cups
   buckwheat flour

about 100g/3½oz/generous
   ¾ cup Italian 00 flour

2 tsp sea salt

1 egg

about 125ml/4fl oz/½ cup
   whole milk

125g/4oz waxy potatoes, cut
   into small cubes

salt and freshly ground
   black pepper

300g/10½oz Savoy cabbage,
   cut into thin strips

100g/3½oz/scant ½ cup
   unsalted butter, plus extra
   for the dish

1 small onion,
   very finely chopped

1 garlic clove,
   very finely chopped

6 fresh sage leaves, torn into
   small pieces

150g/5½oz fontina cheese,
   flaked

75g/2¾oz Parmesan cheese,
   grated

Pizzoccheri are buckwheat pasta made in Valtellina, an Alpine valley in Lombardy. Buckwheat is one of the few crops that grows in this mountainous valley and it is mixed here with the other two local produce, potatoes and cabbage. I have also made pizzoccheri with the green parts of Swiss chard or spring greens. It is a dish full of intense earthy flavours, which, whenever I eat it, takes me back to that beautiful valley, its delicious food and skiing.

On a work surface, mix together the two flours and the salt. Make a well in the middle and break the egg into it. Using a fork, gradually bring in the flour from the wall of the well, while slowly adding the milk. Do not add all the milk at once, since you might not need it all. Depending on the absorbency of the flour or the humidity, you might need to use all the milk, plus a little water, or you might need to add a tablespoon or two more of the white flour. The dough should be soft and elastic, although it is much stickier and wetter than the usual pasta dough. Shape the dough into a ball, wrap it in clingfilm and let it rest for at least 1 hour.

Roll out the dough by hand, or using a pasta machine, to a thickness of 2mm (the last but two notches on the machine). Cut into pappardelle-size strands – 2 x 10cm/¾ x 4 inches – and lay them on clean cloths, not touching each other. (You can do this a day or even two in advance, when the strands will be dry.)

Preheat the oven to 200°C/400°F/gas mark 6. Butter a shallow ovenproof dish.

Put a large saucepan containing about 4 litres/7 pints/4 quarts of water on the heat. Add 1½ tablespoons of salt and the potato and bring to the boil. After about 10 minutes, when the potato cubes begin to soften at the edges, throw in the cabbage and continue cooking for about 5 minutes, until the cabbage has lost its crunchiness. Now slide in the pizzoccheri, mix well and boil for 5–7 minutes.

While this mixture is boiling, heat the butter in a small pan, throw in the onion, garlic and sage and cook gently, stirring frequently, until the onion is pale golden.

When the pizzoccheri are cooked, drain the mixture in a colander and turn it back into the pan. Dress with the butter and onion and mix well.

Using two large forks, transfer about a third of the pasta mixture into the prepared dish. Spread over 2–3 tablespoons of the fontina and Parmesan and plenty of pepper. Cover with another third of the pasta and some of both cheeses, and then a final layer of pasta and cheeses. Cover with foil and bake for about 10 minutes, until the cheeses melt. Serve hot.

Lasagne verdi alla modenese

{ Baked green lasagne }

Serves 4–6

50g/1¾oz/4 tbsp unsalted
butter

1 onion, finely chopped

1 small carrot, finely chopped

1 small celery stalk,
finely chopped

1 garlic clove, finely chopped

100g/3½oz chestnut
(cremini) mushrooms,
chopped

2 tbsp olive oil

100g/3½oz unsmoked
pancetta, cubed

200g/7oz lean minced
(ground) pork

200g/7oz lean minced
(ground) beef

200ml/7fl oz/generous ¾ cup
red wine

2 tbsp tomato purée (paste)
diluted in 4 tbsp water

2 tbsp flat-leaf parsley,
chopped

2 tbsp fresh thyme leaves

salt and freshly ground
black pepper

100–150ml/3½–5½fl oz/
about ½ cup whole milk,
heated

[continues opposite]

This is the traditional variation made in Modena of the classic baked lasagne, the great speciality of Emilia-Romagna. It is usually made with spinach pasta, but plain egg pasta or even dried egg lasagne can be used instead. However, I advise you to spare the time to make your own pasta.

The final result is undoubtedly worth the trouble. If you use the dried lasagne that do not need precooking (which I do not recommend), you will have to make the ragù more liquid and bake the dish for 1 hour.

Heat half the butter in a frying pan and gently sauté the onion, carrot, celery and garlic for about 10–15 minutes, until the vegetables have softened. Throw in the mushrooms and continue cooking for about 5 minutes, stirring frequently. Season with salt.

In a separate saucepan, heat the oil and fry the pancetta for 2 minutes. Add the pork and beef and cook over moderately high heat, breaking up the meat with a fork. When the meat is browned all over, pour in the wine and boil until about half has evaporated. Mix in the diluted tomato purée and cook, stirring, for 1 minute. Add the parsley and thyme and then scoop all the fried vegetables and their juices into the meat sauce. Season with salt and pepper, mix thoroughly and cook, uncovered, over very low heat for about 1½–2 hours. Keep an eye on the ragù and add 2 or 3 tablespoons of hot milk whenever the ragù gets too dry. It is impossible to say exactly how much milk you will need: this depends on, among other things, the heat and the pan you are using.

Preheat the oven to 180°C/350°F/gas mark 4.

To make the lasagne, follow the instructions on page 61, cutting the dough into rectangles measuring about 20 x 10cm/8 x 4 inches. Cook the lasagne in boiling salted water (I use a wide sauté pan) a few sheets at a time, moving them around gently with a fork so they do not stick together; they will take no more than 1–2 minutes. Using a fish slice, lift them out and lay them on clean tea towels while you cook the rest.

To assemble the dish, spread 2–3 tablespoons of the béchamel over the bottom of a 30 x 20cm/12 x 8 inch lasagne dish and cover with a layer of lasagne. Spread over some ragù and 1 or 2 tablespoons of grated Parmesan. Repeat the layers – lasagne, ragù, a little béchamel, Parmesan – until all the

homemade spinach lasagne
(pages 58–61) made with
350g/12 oz Italian 00 flour,
3 eggs and 175g spinach

thick béchamel sauce
(page 74), flavoured with
onion and nutmeg

100g/3½oz Parmesan cheese,
grated

3 tbsp dried white
breadcrumbs

ingredients are used up, finishing with a layer of lasagne. Spread the remaining béchamel all over the top and sprinkle with the remaining Parmesan mixed with the breadcrumbs.

Melt the remaining butter, pour it over the lasagne and bake for about 30 minutes, until the top is golden. Take the dish out of the oven and leave to rest for 2–3 minutes before serving.

Timballo di pasta di Beckendorf

{ Baked pasta with smoked salmon and cheeses }

Serves 6

béchamel sauce (page 74)
made with 750ml milk,
60g unsalted butter
and 50g flour, flavoured
with nutmeg

500g/1lb 2oz farfalle

60g/2¼oz/4½ tbsp unsalted
butter, plus extra for
the dish

250g/9oz smoked salmon,
cut into strips

250g/9oz Gruyère cheese,
sliced

100g/3½oz Parmesan cheese,
grated

3 tbsp dried white
breadcrumbs

salt and freshly ground
black pepper

This delicious dish is attributed to Beckendorf, who was head chef to the Tsar Nicholas II. I have made this timballo more than almost any other and it has always been a success. I use farfalle, certainly not a nineteenth-century pasta, but I find this shape very suitable for the dish.

Preheat the oven to 180°C/350°F/gas mark 4. Butter a baking dish. Make the béchamel sauce and keep warm.

Cook the farfalle in boiling salted water. When just al dente, drain. Melt half the butter and toss with the pasta.

Spoon 2–3 tablespoons of the béchamel into the baking dish. Cover with a third of the pasta, spread over it half the salmon strips, half the Gruyère, 3 tablespoons of Parmesan and 3 tablespoons of béchamel. Repeat these layers, finishing with a layer of pasta. Cover with the remaining béchamel, sprinkle with the remaining Parmesan mixed with the breadcrumbs, and dot with the rest of the butter. Bake for 20–30 minutes, until the top is golden brown. Take the dish out of the oven and leave to rest for 5 minutes before serving.

Il timballo del Gattopardo

{ Sicilian timballo }

Serves 6–8

sweet pastry made with
250g/9oz/2 cups flour

1 cooked chicken (preferably
boiled with vegetables)

1 egg, beaten

100g/3½oz Parmesan cheese,
grated

1 tbsp chopped flat-leaf
parsley

salt and freshly ground
black pepper

2 tbsp Italian 00 flour

vegetable oil for frying

1 tsp wine vinegar

125g/4½oz chicken livers,
trimmed

about 250ml/9fl oz/1 cup
leftover gravy

125g/4½oz prosciutto, cut
into thin strips

1 tsp ground cinnamon

1 white truffle, cleaned
and flaked

250g/9oz macaroni, rigatoni
or penne

125g/4½oz/½ cup unsalted
butter, plus extra for the tin

2 hard-boiled eggs,
cut into segments

1 egg yolk mixed with 2 tbsp
milk, to glaze

This is the most famous baked pasta ever described in literature. It appears in Giuseppe Tomasi di Lampedusa's novel *Il Gattopardo* (The Leopard), set mainly in the 1860s. At a dinner at his country house, the Prince of Salina gives his Sicilian guests a monumental dish of macaroni as a first course, knowing quite well that it would be much more appreciated than a soup of foreign origin. I quote here the description of the timballo, carried into the dining room on a huge silver platter, from the translation by Archibald Colquhoun:

'The burnished gold of the crusts, the fragrance of sugar and cinnamon they exuded, were but preludes to the delights released from the interior when the knife broke the crust: first came a spice-laden haze, the chicken livers, hard-boiled eggs, sliced ham, chicken and truffles in masses of piping hot, glistening macaroni, to which the meat juice gave an exquisite hue of suède.'

The hard-boiled eggs in the timballo were the unlaid eggs that are found inside the chicken, which have a much more delicate flavour.

In his novel, Lampedusa does not give the recipe for the timballo, so this is my interpretation. I am not giving instructions on how to make sweet pastry, since anybody who would attempt to make a dish like this would certainly know how to make sweet pastry.

First make the pastry in your usual way. Wrap it in clingfilm and put it in the fridge.

Remove the meat from the cooked chicken, and finely chop 250g/9oz of the leg meat. In a bowl combine the chopped chicken with the egg, three-quarters of the Parmesan, the parsley, salt and pepper. Mix thoroughly – hands are the best tools – and form the mixture into balls, about the size of a small walnut. Spread the flour on a work surface and roll the meatballs in it to coat them lightly all over. Pour some vegetable oil into a frying pan to come about 1cm/½ inch up the sides of the pan, place over medium–high heat, and, when very hot, slide in the meatballs. Fry for 5 minutes, turning them over halfway through. When all are nice and brown, lift them out and drain on kitchen paper. Set aside.

Cut the chicken breast meat into thin strips and set aside.

Bring a small pan of water to the boil, add some salt and the vinegar and blanch the chicken livers for 2 minutes. Drain and chop them.

Heat the gravy in a saucepan and, if necessary, boil until slightly reduced. Add the chicken breast, chicken livers and prosciutto and cook gently for a few minutes. The sauce should be thick and velvety. Add the cinnamon and truffle, and adjust the seasoning to taste.

Preheat the oven to 200°C/400°F/gas mark 6. Butter a 20cm/8 inch springform tin.

Drop the macaroni into rapidly boiling salted water.

Meanwhile, roll out the pastry and cut out two discs, one with a diameter of 20cm/8 inches, the other about 35cm/14 inches. Lay the larger disc in the prepared tin, so that the pastry comes up the sides of the tin. Use the rolled-out pastry trimmings to cut out some decorations for the top of the pie.

When the macaroni is very al dente, drain, return it to the pan in which it has cooked and toss with the butter. Spoon in the chicken and ham sauce, mix thoroughly and then add the remaining Parmesan and mix again.

Spoon about three-quarters of the pasta into the pastry-lined tin. Make a well in the centre, and put into it the meatballs and hard-boiled eggs. Cover neatly with the remaining pasta and then with the smaller disc of pastry. Make some holes all over the top of the pie with a fork, add the pastry decorations and then brush with the egg yolk mixture. Bake for about 1 hour, or until the pastry is cooked and golden brown. Leave the timballo to cool in the tin for about 10 minutes, then turn it out onto a round dish and serve.

Stuffed pasta

Of all pasta dishes the following recipes for stuffed pasta are, without doubt, the most complex to make. Any kind of stuffed pasta requires quite a lot of time as well. However, the result is very rewarding, both to the palate and to the eye, and any child would love to help you.

Rotolo di spinaci

{ Pasta roll with spinach filling }

Serves 6

homemade pasta dough
(pages 58–61) made with
200g/7oz Italian 00 flour
and 2 eggs

300g/10½oz cooked spinach
or frozen leaf spinach,
thawed

salt and freshly ground
black pepper

50g/1¾oz/4 tbsp unsalted
butter, plus extra for the
dish

1 garlic clove, lightly crushed

250g/9oz/1 cup ricotta

a generous grating of nutmeg

1 egg yolk

béchamel sauce (page 74)

100g/3½oz Parmesan cheese,
grated

2 tbsp dried breadcrumbs

A very attractive, delicious and different dish, which is always a success.
It takes a bit of time and care in the making, but it is well worth the effort.

It is difficult to state the precise quantity of raw spinach you need to start
with, because it depends so much on the type of spinach: with some kinds you
can use everything, with others you have to discard the tough larger stems. So
here I give the weight of the cooked spinach.

Make the pasta dough following the instructions on pages 58–61. Wrap in
clingfilm and leave to rest while you make the filling.

If you are using fresh spinach, wash it in plenty of cold water, put it in a
saucepan with 1 teaspoon of salt, but without adding any water, cover and cook
over high heat for 3–4 minutes, until tender. If you are using frozen spinach,
cook in a covered pan with 1 teaspoon of salt for about 2 minutes. Drain the
spinach, leave to cool and then squeeze it gently with your hands to get rid of all
the liquid. Chop coarsely.

In a frying pan, heat half the butter with the garlic, add the spinach and sauté
gently for 5 minutes. Remove the garlic and transfer the spinach to a bowl. Add
the ricotta, nutmeg and egg yolk. Mix thoroughly, taste and adjust the seasoning.

Roll out the pasta dough as thin as you can, into a rectangle measuring about
50 x 30cm/20 x 12 inches. Trim the sides neatly, using a long sharp knife, and
then spread the spinach filling over the pasta, leaving a 2.5cm/1 inch border
all round. Fold one of the long edges over the filling, and continue to fold and
roll until you have a log shape. Wrap the roll tightly in a piece of muslin or
cheesecloth, and tie the two ends securely with string, so that it looks like a large
Christmas cracker.

Take a fish kettle or an oval pan, large enough to hold the pasta roll, and fill with water, add 1 tablespoon of salt and bring to the boil. When the water comes to the boil, turn down the heat and gently lower the roll into the water. Cover the pan and simmer very gently for about 25–30 minutes. Lift the pasta roll carefully out of the water and place on a board, cover with a dish and leave to cool. (It is easier to slice when cold.)

Preheat the oven to 180°C/350°F/gas mark 4. Butter a shallow baking dish. Make the béchamel and add the Parmesan.

Cut the pasta roll into slices about 2cm/¾ inch thick. Lay the slices in the baking dish in a single layer, overlapping them slightly. Melt the remaining butter in a small saucepan and pour it over the slices. Spread the béchamel evenly over the top, sprinkle with the breadcrumbs and bake for about 30 minutes. If you like, finish the dish under a hot grill for a few minutes before serving.

Variations

• *Instead of covering the slices with béchamel, melt 100g/3½oz of unsalted butter with 2 lightly crushed garlic cloves. Remove the garlic and pour the butter over the slices, and then sprinkle with 75g/2¾oz of grated Parmesan. Bake as above.*

• *Instead of béchamel, spoon over some plain tomato sauce (page 72) and then dot with 50g/1¾oz/4 tbsp of unsalted butter. Bake as above.*

Ravioli alla milanese

{ Meat ravioli }

Serves 4–5

homemade pasta dough
(pages 58–61) made with
300g/10½oz Italian 00 flour
and 3 eggs

50g/1¾oz/4 tbsp unsalted
butter

7–8 fresh sage leaves, torn
into pieces

1 garlic clove, lightly crushed

40g/1½oz/6 tbsp Parmesan
cheese, grated, plus extra
to serve

Stuffing

50g/1¾oz/4 tbsp unsalted
butter

a sprig of rosemary

250g/9oz braising steak,
such as chuck,
cut into pieces

125ml/4fl oz/½ cup red wine

2–3 tbsp meat stock

salt and freshly ground
black pepper

60g/2¼oz prosciutto,
cut into small bits

1 egg

2 tbsp freshly grated
Parmesan cheese

a generous pinch of ground
cinnamon

Ravioli are made in every region of northern and central Italy. This is one of the classic recipes, as made in Milan and as they were made in my home. You will need thickly cut prosciutto, not the thin pre-packed slices.

Make the pasta dough following the instructions on pages 58–61. Wrap in clingfilm and leave to rest while you make the stuffing.

In a saucepan, heat half the butter with the rosemary. Add the beef and brown it quickly on all sides over moderate heat. Reduce the heat and pour in the wine. Let it bubble away for 2–3 minutes and then add the stock. Season with salt and pepper and cook, covered, over very low heat for about 1½ hours, or until the meat is tender. You may have to add a few tablespoons of hot water during the cooking if the sauce becomes too dry. Leave to cool slightly.

Spoon the pieces of meat into a food processor and pulse until the meat is very finely chopped, but be careful not to reduce it to a paste. Transfer the meat to a bowl and mix in the prosciutto, egg, Parmesan and cinnamon. Taste and adjust the seasoning. Add enough of the meat cooking liquid to make the mixture quite damp but not dripping with liquid.

Cut off a quarter of the pasta dough, leaving the rest wrapped in clingfilm. Roll out the dough by hand or by machine (see p. 61). If using a machine, roll until you get to the second to last notch. If rolling by hand, roll the dough as thin as you can and then cut into long strips, about 13–15cm/5–6 inches wide. Working quickly to avoid the pasta drying out, lay out a strip in front of you. Place teaspoonfuls of the stuffing onto the strip in a straight line at 5cm/2 inch intervals, 5cm/2 inches from the cut edge. Fold the dough lengthwise over the stuffing and, using a pastry wheel or a sharp knife, trim the edge where the dough meets. Cut into squares between each mound of stuffing. Separate the squares and gently squeeze out any air that may be caught in the ravioli. Seal the cut edges tightly, with moistened fingers, and set aside on a clean tea towel. Continue making the ravioli until you have used up all the filling or the dough.

Preheat the oven to 120°C/250°F/gas mark ½.

Melt the butter in a small saucepan. Add the sage leaves, the garlic, and the remaining cooking juices (removing the rosemary). Stir for 1 minute, remove the garlic and pour the butter sauce into a serving bowl. Add the Parmesan and put the bowl into the oven to keep warm while you cook the ravioli.

Drop the ravioli gently into a large saucepan of boiling salted water. Stir gently and cook over moderate heat – the water should not boil fast, or they might break – for about 4 minutes. The best way to tell if they are ready is to try one: the pasta round the edge should be cooked but still al dente. Drain the ravioli and turn them into the warmed serving bowl. Toss them in the sauce and serve at once, handing around a bowl of grated Parmesan.

Conchiglioni ripieni di ricotta

{ Big pasta shells stuffed with ricotta }

Serves 4

250g/9oz conchiglioni

4 tbsp unsalted butter, plus extra for the dish

1 garlic clove, lightly crushed

6 sage leaves, torn into pieces

150ml/5fl oz/⅔ cup double (heavy) cream

50g/1¾oz Parmesan, grated

Stuffing

1 slice of crustless white bread, soaked in milk

125g/4½oz ricotta

1 egg

50g/1¾oz Parmesan, grated

4 tbsp chopped flat-leaf parsley

a generous grating of nutmeg

¼ tsp ground cinnamon

salt and ground black pepper

a little semolina

This stuffing can also be used with cannelloni (page 191).

Preheat the oven to 180°C/350°F/gas mark 4. Butter a large, shallow baking dish.

Drop the pasta shells into rapidly boiling salted water and cook according to the packet instructions. Drain well.

While the pasta is cooking, make the stuffing. Squeeze the milk from the bread. Combine the bread with the ricotta, egg, Parmesan, parsley, nutmeg, cinnamon, salt and pepper and mix together very thoroughly.

Fill each pasta shell with a little of the mixture and sprinkle the top with semolina. (The semolina acts as a seal.) Lay the shells in the baking dish.

In a small saucepan, melt the butter with the garlic and the sage; when the butter starts to colour, mix in the cream. Cook, stirring constantly, for 30 seconds and then remove the garlic and pour the sauce all over the shells. Cover with foil and bake for about 15 minutes. Serve the remaining Parmesan in a bowl on the side.

Variation
Omit the nutmeg and cinnamon in the ricotta mixture. Mix in 1 very finely chopped garlic clove and 4 tablespoons of chopped flat-leaf parsley. Fill the shells with this mixture and cover with plain tomato sauce (page 72) before baking.

Ravioli di magro

{ Ravioli with spinach and ricotta }

Serves 4

homemade pasta dough
   (pages 58–61) made with
   200g/7oz Italian 00 flour
   and 2 eggs

300g/10½oz fresh young
   spinach or 300g/10½oz
   frozen spinach, thawed

125g/4½oz/½ cup ricotta

1 egg

45g/1½oz/4 tbsp sultanas
   (golden raisins)

1 tsp ground cinnamon

½ tsp freshly grated nutmeg

salt and freshly ground
   black pepper

50g/1¾oz/4 tbsp unsalted
   butter, melted

50g/1¾oz Parmesan cheese,
   grated, to serve

This is my adaptation of the first recipe for ravioli – *Rafioli comun de herbe vantazati*, 'common ravioli with leaves'. It is from a collection of recipes by an unknown Venetian – '*anonimo veneziano*' – who was writing in the late fourteenth and early fifteenth century. *Ravioli di magro* – 'ravioli for a meatless day' – are still made in the same way.

'If you want to make ravioli with leaves, pick some leaves, clean them well and wash them. Boil them a little, take them out and squeeze them well and cut them with the knife and then pound them in the mortar. And take some fresh cheese and some sour cheese and eggs and sweet and spicy spices and sultanas and mix well together and make a paste. And then make a thin *sfoglia* and take little pieces of the mixture and make the ravioli. When they are made, cook them, and when they are cooked powder them on top with an abundant quantity of spices and with good cheese and butter. And they are very good.'

Make the pasta dough following the instructions on pages 58–61. Wrap in clingfilm and leave to rest while you make the stuffing.

If you are using fresh spinach, wash it in plenty of cold water, put it in a saucepan without adding any water, cover and cook over high heat for 3–4 minutes, until just wilted. Drain in a colander and as soon as it is cool enough to handle, squeeze all the water out of the spinach using your hands. If you are using frozen spinach, just squeeze it out. Chop the spinach coarsely and put it into a bowl.

Add the ricotta, egg, sultanas, cinnamon, nutmeg, salt and pepper. Mix very well – hands are the best tools – and then taste and adjust the seasoning.

Roll out the dough and make the ravioli as for Ravioli alla milanese (page 188), using the spinach stuffing.

Drop the ravioli gently into a large saucepan of boiling salted water. The water should not boil too fast, or the ravioli might break. Cook for about 4–5 minutes and then lift them out using a slotted spoon and put them into a warmed serving dish. Pour over the melted butter and serve with a bowl of grated Parmesan on the side.

Cannelloni ripieni alla piemontese

{ Cannelloni stuffed with meat }

Serves 6–8

homemade pasta dough
  (pages 58–61) made with
  300g/10½oz Italian 00 flour
  and 3 eggs, or 18 sheets of
  dried egg lasagne

béchamel sauce (p. 74) made
  with 600ml milk, 50g butter
  and 40–45g flour, flavoured
  with nutmeg

30g/1oz Parmesan cheese,
  grated

1 tbsp unsalted butter, plus
  extra for the bowl

Stuffing

5 tbsp olive oil

a sprig of rosemary

1 small onion, finely chopped

250g/9oz minced (ground)
  beef

125g/4½oz luganega or other
  coarse sausage, skin off

salt and ground black pepper

150ml/5fl oz/⅔ cup red or
  dry white wine

2 tbsp tomato purée (paste),
  diluted in 2 tbsp water

100ml/3½fl oz/scant ½ cup
  whole milk

2 eggs

30g/1oz Parmesan cheese,
  grated

Cannelloni can be stuffed with various meat mixtures, of which this is one of the most common, or with spinach and ricotta. This dish can be prepared in advance, but do not cover the cannelloni with béchamel sauce until just before you bake them.

If you are making the pasta at home, follow the instructions on pages 58–61. Wrap in clingfilm and leave to rest while you make the stuffing.

To make the stuffing, heat the oil in a saucepan and sauté the rosemary for 2–3 minutes, then fish it out and discard it. Add the onion, sauté for 5 minutes and then add the beef and sausage. Brown well, breaking up the lumps of meat with a fork. Taste and add some salt and pepper. Pour in the wine and let it bubble away until the liquid has reduced by two-thirds. Mix in the diluted tomato purée, stir for 1 minute, add a little of the milk and then turn down the heat and simmer for at least 1 hour. Keep an eye on it; you might have to add some more milk if the ragù looks very dry, but at the end of the cooking time you want a pretty dry ragù, drier than the one you make for tagliatelle.When the ragù is done, tip it into a mixing bowl and leave to cool. When cool, mix in the eggs, one at a time, and the Parmesan. Taste and adjust the seasoning. Set aside.

Preheat the oven to 190°C/375°F/gas mark 5.

Roll out the pasta dough as thin as you can and cut into lasagne sheets – rectangles measuring about 20 x 10cm/8 x 4 inches.

Cook the lasagne in boiling salted water a few sheets at a time (I use a wide sauté pan), moving them around gently with a fork so they do not stick together. If homemade, they will take no more than 1–2 minutes; if dried, start testing 2 minutes before the time suggested on the packet. When they are still a little hard to the bite, lift them out and lay them on tea towels while you cook the rest.

Generously butter a lasagne dish, large enough to hold all the cannelloni in a single layer. Spread 2 tablespoons of the meat mixture on each rectangle of pasta, leaving a 2cm/¾ inch border all round. Roll the strip up its narrow side and place in the dish with the folded-over edge facing downwards. You can pack the cannelloni together tightly but they must all be in a single layer.

Spread the béchamel over the top, sprinkle with the Parmesan and dot with the butter. Bake for 20 minutes. Take the dish out of the oven and leave to rest for about 5 minutes before serving.

Timballo di anolini alla Piacentina

{ Timballo of anolini stuffed with braised beef }

Serves 8

sweet pastry made with
   450g flour

homemade pasta dough
   (pages 58–61) made with
   300g/10½oz Italian 00 flour
   and 3 eggs

50g/1¾oz/4 tbsp unsalted
   butter

50g/1¾oz Parmesan cheese,
   grated, plus extra to serve

1 egg yolk mixed with 1 tsp
   cold water, to glaze

Stuffing

1 small piece of braising beef,
   preferably brisket,
   weighing approximately
   500g/1lb 2oz

2 tbsp olive oil

50g/1¾oz/4 tbsp unsalted
   butter

1 onion, very finely chopped

1 carrot, very finely chopped

1 small celery stalk, very
   finely chopped

1 garlic clove, finely chopped

250ml/9fl oz/1 cup red wine

[continues opposite]

This is quite a time-consuming dish to make, but the end result looks marvellous and tastes delicious. I am not giving instructions on how to make the sweet pastry; follow your usual recipe, starting with 450g flour.

First make the pastry in your usual way. Wrap it in clingfilm and put it in the fridge.

In a small heavy-bottomed casserole, just big enough to hold the meat comfortably, heat the oil and butter and add the onion, carrot, celery and garlic. Cook until the vegetables soften, about 10 minutes, stirring frequently. Lift out the vegetables using a slotted spoon and set aside. Put the meat into the pan, turn up the heat and brown quickly on all sides. Now pour in the wine and boil rapidly until the liquid is almost completely evaporated. Put the vegetables back into the pan and add the tomato purée and half the stock. Turn the heat down, cover the pan and cook very gently for about 2 hours, until the meat is tender. Add a little more stock if necessary, but not much, because at the end of the cooking time the juice should be thick. Add 3 tablespoons of water to the casserole and set aside. You can cook the meat a day or two in advance and chill it.

Make the pasta dough following the instructions on pages 58–59. Wrap in clingfilm and leave to rest while you finish the stuffing.

In a bowl, soak the breadcrumbs in some of the meat juice. Finely chop the meat and add to the breadcrumbs. Add the eggs, cheese and nutmeg, salt and pepper and stir until well blended – hands are the best tools. Set aside.

Now you are ready to make the anolini. Roll out the pasta dough by hand or by machine (see pages 60–61). If using a pasta machine, cut off a piece of dough about the size of an orange, leaving the rest wrapped in clingfilm, and pass it through the rollers until you get to the last but one notch; roll out one strip at a time. If you are rolling out by hand, cut off about a third of the dough and roll out as thin as you can. Using a 5cm/2 inch diameter fluted cutter, cut out as many discs as you can. Place a small teaspoonful of the stuffing in the middle of each disc. Lightly moisten around the edge of the disc with cold water, then fold the dough over the stuffing to make a crescent shape, and press down the edges with damp fingers. Gather together all the cut-up bits of dough and push them back into the remaining dough, which you must keep wrapped in clingfilm.

1 tbsp tomato purée (paste)

250ml/9fl oz/1 cup meat
  stock or bouillon

75g/2¾oz/1⅔ cups fresh
  white breadcrumbs

2 eggs

50g/1¾oz Parmesan cheese,
  grated

a grating of nutmeg

salt and freshly ground
  black pepper

Repeat the rolling, cutting and filling until you have used all the pasta dough. Set the anolini out in rows on clean tea towels. If you are not using them straight away, turn them over very couple of hours or so, until they are dry all over.

Preheat the oven to 180°C/350°F/gas mark 4. Butter a 25cm/10 inch springform tin.

Drop the anolini gently into a large saucepan of boiling salted water. Stir gently and cook over moderate heat – the water should not boil fast or the anolini might break – for about 4–5 minutes. It might be easier to cook them in batches. Lift them out of the water using a slotted spoon, put them into a bowl, and dry them with kitchen paper. Dress them with the butter and Parmesan.

Put the casserole in which the meat has been cooked over high heat and bring to the boil, scraping the bottom of the pan with a spoon to release the cooking residue. Boil for a minute or two and then pour over the anolini. Place the bowl with the anolini at the bottom of the oven.

Take the pastry out of the fridge. Cut off about a third of it and roll out into a 25cm/10 inch diameter disc; lay the pastry disc on the bottom of the buttered springform tin. Cut off another third of the pastry and roll out strips of pastry to line the sides of the tin. Press well to seal the pastry sides to the base and then spoon the anolini and all the juices into the pastry case. Do not press down – the anolini should be quite loose. If you have too many, keep the leftovers for another occasion (they are delicious in a meat stock).

Roll out the remaining pastry into a disc to fit the top of the tin. Place over the anolini and press the edges to seal. Using a fork, prick some holes in the top, and then brush the top with the egg yolk mixture. Cut out some shapes from the rolled-out pastry trimmings to decorate the top of the pie and brush them lightly with the glaze.

Bake for 50–60 minutes, until the pastry is cooked and golden brown. Leave to cool in the tin for 10 minutes, then run a thin knife between the tin and the pastry and carefully release the spring clips. Serve hot, with a bowl of grated Parmesan.

Tortellini di ricotta e erbe aromatiche

{ Tortellini filled with ricotta and sweet herbs }

**Serves 4–6; allow about
16–20 tortellini per person**

homemade pasta dough
(pages 58–61) made with
300g/10½oz Italian 00 flour
and 3 eggs

30g/1oz parsley, sage,
marjoram, chives or other
fresh herbs

300g/10½oz/1¼ cups ricotta

a generous grating of nutmeg,
about 1 tsp

1 egg yolk

100g/3½oz Parmesan cheese,
grated

salt and freshly ground
black pepper

Tortellini are usually stuffed with meat (you can use the stuffing for anolini on page 192 or for ravioli alla milanese on page 188), but my favourite tortellini are these, stuffed with ricotta and herbs. The herbs can be a mixture of your favourites, but the essential two are parsley and sage.

These delicate tortellini are best dressed in the simplest ways. You can gently melt some butter until golden with a crushed garlic clove and some chopped sage leaves, or use the dressing for tagliatelle all'inglese or fettuccine all'Alfredo (page 128). During the truffle season, finish them off as you would a dish of tajerin (page 161).

Make the pasta dough following the instructions on pages 58–61. Wrap in clingfilm and leave to rest while you make the stuffing.

Chop all the herbs until very fine and put in a bowl. Add all the other ingredients and mix very thoroughly. Taste and adjust the seasoning. Set aside.

Roll out the dough by hand or by machine (see pages 60–61). If using a pasta machine, cut off a piece of pasta dough about the size of an orange, leaving the rest wrapped in clingfilm, and pass it through the rollers until you get to the last notch; roll out one strip at a time. If you are rolling out by hand, cut off about a quarter of the dough and roll out as thin as you can.

Using a small cutter (about 3cm/1¼ inch diameter) or a liqueur glass, cut out discs of pasta dough.

Place half a teaspoon of the filling in the middle of each disc, fold over half of the disc to form a half moon shape, with the upper edge about 3mm shorter on meeting the lower. Press down firmly to seal and then pick up the half moon with the round edge facing upwards and wrap it around your index finger. Press the extremities firmly together with your thumb, and then lay the shapes out on clean tea towels. Gather together all the cut-up bits of dough and press them together to be re-rolled. Go on with this labour of love until all the pasta dough is transformed into edible navels.

The rest is easy. Boil the tortellini in a large saucepan of salted boiling water. I recommend cooking them in two batches and in water that is boiling steadily, but not too fast, or they might break. When done – about 4–5 minutes – lift out the first batch with a slotted spoon, place in a serving dish, pat dry with kitchen paper, dot with a little butter and keep warm in a low oven. When you have cooked all the tortellini, dress them (see recipe introduction) and serve at once – you will be amply rewarded for your labour.

Sweet
pasta dishes

Pasta was often eaten as a 'pudding' up to the
eighteenth century in Italy and even later in
America and in England. There are also a few
Central European recipes that use pasta in sweet
dishes. You might like to try them, and you will
realize that pasta is certainly one of the most
versatile of foods.

Dolce di capelli d'angelo al cioccolato

{ Angel's hair and chocolate cake }

Serves 8

100g/3½oz dark chocolate
(minimum 70% cocoa
solids), cut into
small pieces

150ml/5fl oz/ ⅔ cup single
(light) cream

2 tbsp caster (superfine)
sugar

200g/7oz capelli d'angelo
(very fine pasta strands)

100g/3½oz/¾ cup blanched
almonds, chopped

50g/1¾oz/½ cup walnut
halves, chopped

3 tbsp clear honey

grated rind of 1½ unwaxed
lemons

1 tsp ground cinnamon

a pinch of salt

This is one of the few traditional Italian sweet pasta dishes. It comes from Orvieto in Umbria and it is good. In Umbria this dish is served as it is, but I find that a jug of cream is quite welcome.

Put the chocolate in a small saucepan, add the cream and the sugar and heat very slowly until the chocolate has melted, stirring the whole time.

Cook the pasta in lightly salted boiling water and drain it about 1 minute after the water returns to the boil, when it is just slightly undercooked, reserving a cupful of the water. Pour the chocolate sauce over the pasta and stir thoroughly, adding some 1 or 2 tablespoons of the reserved pasta water.

Wash and dry the small saucepan. Mix all the other ingredients together in the cleaned saucepan, keeping aside 2 tablespoons of the walnuts. Heat very gently until all the nuts are coated with honey.

Lay half the capelli d'angelo in a buttered 1 litre/1¾ pint/4 cup baking dish. Spread the nut mixture evenly over it and then top with the remaining pasta. Scatter the remaining walnuts over the top and place in the fridge for at least 2 hours.

Take the pudding out of the fridge some time before serving, as it is best eaten at room temperature.

Tagliatelle al cioccolato

{ Chocolate tagliatelle }

Serves 4–5

Chocolate tagliatelle

150–225g/5½–8oz/
 1¼–1¾ cups Italian 00 flour

50g/1¾oz/scant ½ cup best-
 quality unsweetened cocoa
 powder, sifted

a pinch of fine sea salt

2 eggs and 1 yolk

Caramel pecan sauce

30g/1oz/2 tbsp unsalted
 butter

3 heaped tbsp muscovado
 sugar

50g/1¾oz/½ cup pecans,
 chopped

6 tbsp single (light) cream,
 plus extra to serve

Certainly not a dish from the past: these chocolate tagliatelle were created by me for a cookery demonstration at a food fair intended to appeal to children. It was a great success in spite of the weather – wet, windy and cold, a typical ghastly summer day in Dorset.

Make the tagliatelle following the instructions on pages 58–61, first mixing the cocoa into the flour.

For the sauce, melt the butter over very low heat and mix in the sugar. Stir frequently until all the sugar is melted, and then add the pecans. Mix to coat the nuts in the caramel and then slowly pour in the cream. Set aside.

Cook the pasta in lightly salted boiling water, drain and dress immediately with the hot caramel sauce. Serve with extra cream on the side.

Cataif

{ *Sweet noodles with raisins and almonds* }

Serves 6–8

homemade tagliatelle
    (pages 58–61) made with
    250g/9oz Italian 00 flour,
    2 eggs and 2 tablespoons
    water, or 250g/9oz dried
    egg tagliatelle

85g/3oz/6 tbsp unsalted
    butter

2 tsp ground cinnamon

85g/3oz/½ cup raisins

100g/3½oz/¾ cup almonds,
    blanched, toasted
    and chopped

40g/1½oz/4 tbsp mixed peel

grated rind of 1 unwaxed
    lemon

40g/1½oz/3 tbsp caster
    (superfine) sugar

salt

double (heavy) cream,
    to serve

Caramel topping

100g/3½oz/½ cup caster
    (superfine) sugar

4 tbsp cold water

juice of 1 lemon

This is an old Romanian recipe, a delicious and esoteric pudding which should be made with homemade pasta.

If you are making the pasta at home, follow the instructions on pages 58–61, adding the water to the eggs before mixing in the flour.

Preheat the oven to 150°C/300°F/gas mark 2. Butter a baking dish.

Drop the tagliatelle into rapidly boiling water to which you have added 1 tablespoon of salt. If you are using homemade pasta, drain it 2 minutes after the water returns to the boil. If using dried tagliatelle, drain when it is very al dente. Toss immediately with 50g/1¾oz/4 tablespoons of the butter and sprinkle with the cinnamon.

Transfer a third of the pasta into the baking dish, cover with half the raisins, almonds, mixed peel, lemon rind and sugar. Repeat these layers, and finish with pasta. Dot with the remaining butter and bake for 20 minutes.

While the pasta is baking, make the caramel topping. Put the sugar into a saucepan and stir over low heat until the sugar melts and turns golden brown. Take off the heat and add the water. Take care, because the mixture will boil furiously when the water is added. Return the pan to the heat and stir until syrupy. Add the lemon juice. Pour this sauce over the pasta, and bake the pudding for an additional 5 minutes. Serve hot, with cream on the side.

Lokshen shalet

{ Noodle and apple cake }

Serves 6

homemade tagliatelle/
tagliolini (pages 58–61)
made with 200g/7oz
Italian 00 flour and 2 eggs,
or 250g/9oz dried egg
tagliatelle

125g/4½oz/¾ cup raisins

4 tbsp rum

75g/2¾oz/5 tbsp unsalted
butter, plus extra for
the dish

3 eggs, separated

100g/3½oz/½ cup caster
(superfine) sugar

2 tsp ground cinnamon

a pinch of ground cloves

a generous grating of nutmeg

500g/1lb 2oz tart eating
apples, peeled and
finely sliced

double (heavy) cream,
to serve

This traditional Jewish pudding originated in Germany, but it migrated to Poland, as indeed a lot of Jewish people did.

If you are making the pasta at home, follow the instructions on pages 58–61.

Preheat the oven to 180°C/350°F/gas mark 4. Butter a deep baking dish. Soak the raisins in the rum.

Cook the tagliatelle in lightly salted boiling water. If you are using homemade tagliatelle, drain it 2 minutes after the water returns to the boil. If using dried tagliatelle, drain when it is very al dente. Toss immediately with 50g/1¾oz/ 4 tablespoons of the butter.

Lightly beat the egg yolks and add to the pasta, together with the sugar, raisins and rum, and the spices. Whip the egg whites until stiff and fold them into the mixture.

Spoon half of the mixture into the baking dish. Lay the apple slices on top and cover with the remaining mixture. Dot with the remaining butter, cover with foil, and bake for about 30 minutes. Serve hot, with the cream.

Index

First published in the United Kingdom in 2015 by
Pavilion
An imprint of HarperCollinsPublishers
1 London Bridge Street
London SE1 9GF

www.harpercollins.co.uk

HarperCollinsPublishers
Macken House
39/40 Mayor Street Upper
Dublin 1
D01 C9W8
Ireland

This book is produced from independently certified FSC™
paper to ensure responsible forest management.
For more information visit:
www.harpercollins.co.uk/green

ISBN: 978-1-90981-562-9

Commissioning Editors: Rebecca Spry and Emily Preece-
Morrison
Copy Editor: Maggie Ramsay
Illustrator: Alison Legg
Picture Research: Emily Hedges
Design Concept and Cover: Laura Russell
Layout Designer: Maru Studio

A CIP catalogue record for this book is available from the
British Library.
10 9 8 7 6 5 4

Reproduction by Mission Productions, Hong Kong(China) and
Rival Colour Ltd, United Kingdom
Printed and bound by RRD Ltd., China

www.pavilionbooks.com

Picture Credits
The Publisher would like to thank the following sources for
their kind permission to reproduce images in this book:
Image Courtesy of The Advertising Archives: p.37, akg-images/
ullstein bild/Alfred Eisenstae: p.30, Alamy/©Nigel Cattlin: p.9,
© BBC photo Library: p.42, Bridgeman Images: /Alinari p.23, /
De Agostini Picture Library/L. Pedicini p.21, /Bibliotheque
des Arts Decoratifs, Paris, France/Archives Charmet
p.24, /Musee des Beaux-Arts, Mulhouse, France p.32, /
Osterreichische
Nationalbibliothek, Vienna, Austria/Alinari p.19, /Private
Collection/© Look and Learn/Peter Jackson Collection p.35,
/Private
Collection/The Stapleton Collection p.15 b, © The
British Library Board: p.17, Corbis: /©Bettmann p.29.
/©GraphicaArtis p.8,
©Fratelli Alinari /Fosco Maraini/Proprietà Gabinetto
Vieusseux: p.14, Getty Images: /Hulton Archive p.13 b, /Photo
Ronald
Startup/Picture Post p.44-45, Mary Evans Picture Library: p.13
t, p.15 t, /©Illustrated London News Ltd. p.11, /Retrograph
Collection p.36 t and b.
17207_